Baptism in Water and Baptism in the Spirit

A Biblical, Liturgical, and Theological Exposition

Philippe Larere, O.P.

translated by
Patrick Madigan, O.S.B.

A Liturgical Press Book

 THE LITURGICAL PRESS
Collegeville, Minnesota

Cover design by Nathan Owen-Block

This book was originally published in French as *Baptême dans l'Esprit et Baptême d'Eau: Une présentation biblique, liturgique, et théologique* by Editions du Lion de Juda/Pneumathèque, La Société des Oeuvres Communautaires, Burtin, 41600 Nouan le Fuzelier, France. Copyright © 1991 Pneumathèque, Société des Oeuvres Communautaires.

1	2	3	4	5	6	7	8

Library of Congress Cataloging-in-Publication Data

Larere, Philippe.
  [Baptême dans l'Esprit et baptême d'eau.   English]
  Baptism in water and baptism in the Spirit : a biblical,
liturgical, and theological exposition / Philippe Larere ;
translated by Patrick Madigan.
      p.   cm.
  ISBN 0-8146-2225-9
  1. Baptism. 2. Baptism in the Holy Spirit. 3. Infant baptism.
  4. Baptism and church membership. 5. Baptism and Christian union.
  I. Title.
BV811.2.L3713   1993
234'.161—dc20   93-10845
                                                              CIP

Contents

Introduction

Baptism in Water and Baptism in the Spirit. . . . Such is the title of this work. The careful reader would benefit from a definition of each at the outset, so that the one may be distinguished from the other and their differences clearly established.

Unfortunately, our approach must be longer and more circuitous if we truly hope to throw some light on this expression "baptism in the Spirit" in the sense that Pentacostals and Charismatics use it today. We must rather begin our study with the Word of God, for it is there that we must explore what the word "baptism" means in the Gospels and in the Acts of the Apostles.

The Churches themselves, at least certain of them, will then provide for our consideration their own practices of baptism and the doctrines by which they support them. Only then may we cast a cursory glance over the issues that have led certain among them to baptize infants (or not) or to "rebaptize" (or not) a Christian joining their own community. We will then finally be in a position to appreciate what baptism in the spirit is for each tradition and understand its connection with baptism in water.

The purpose of this work is thus not to develop the opinions of the author on this topic, as original and interesting as these might be, but rather the more modest one of providing the reader with the necessary elements to pose this question correctly, and thereby to free oneself from many intractable and fruitless entanglements on this fundamental issue in the Christian faith.

We hope that these pages will be judged according to this ambition.

CHAPTER ONE

The Word of God

WE ARE ALL SINNERS

"If with your mouth you confess that Jesus is Lord and if in your heart you believe that God raised him from the dead, you will be saved" (Rom 10:9). Thus, according to the Apostle Paul, to be saved, that is, to escape the condemnation weighing on every human being (that is, "since you have disobeyed, you will die"), and to have some part in the glory of God, one must affirm before the whole world that Jesus is Lord and believe in one's heart that God led him back from death to life.

But has not every human being disobeyed, that is, refused to carry out God's will?

Paul states: "We have already made it clear: everyone, both Jew and Greek alike, is under the reign of sin" (Rom 3:9), which means: I have already shown that all men find themselves in the grip of sin.

Our human experience confirms this. The baby, instinctively, is an egoist: it operates on its own behalf and opposes the legitimate will of its parents. Having reached what is called the age of reason at about six or seven years, one day the child does something for which his or her conscience reproaches the child: having become capable by that experience of distinguishing good from evil, the child becomes conscious of the fact that he or she is indeed a sinner. And even the most mature adolescent, who by and large does what he or she should, sometimes does something he or she shouldn't. And even the most upright man or woman has their weaknesses.

In this way the most complete moral integrity will not keep one from succumbing to temptation: "I can will the good," writes Paul, "but not carry it out, for the good that I wish, I do not, but the evil that I do not wish, that I do" (Rom 7:18-19). Even if he has the desire to do what is right, one does not reach the point of actually doing it.

Why is it this way? Why does sin repeat itself from generation to generation due to the fact that a person, in awaking to moral awareness at the "age of reason," commits his or her first sin, the one that reveals that the person is a sinner?

Paul says correctly: "It is not I who act, but sin that lives in me" (Rom 7:20). Otherwise expressed: within me there exist evil tendencies which push me to sin; and they are so strong and deeply rooted in me that sooner or later they will exceed my powers of resistance. Each person walks around like an invalid who cannot even conquer his or her own bacteria. But where does such an inclination to commit evil come from?

Paul explains it thus: "Just as through one man sin entered the world, and with sin death, and thus all men taste death, for all have sinned. . . ." (Rom 5:12); Paul does not bring his sentence to an end, there, for even that is not the precise point he wishes to develop. That is why this text has been the subject for so many commentaries. At the very least we can interpret it as saying that sin entered the world because of one man, Adam, and that sin leads to death; and also, death is part of the fate of everyone, for all have sinned.

Let us develop this point some more. As far back as one chooses to go in human history, the first man, even if we are dealing with a being little distinct from an animal, and even if there were several of them, still had to choose between good and evil, in accord with the intention of his Creator who gave him the gift of liberty. Just like today's adolescent with regard to one's first sin, one day realizes that he or she has not kept to his or her status as a creature, for by deciding what was good for oneself has appropriated a role reserved for the Creator. This act has immediate and long lasting consequences: from now on there are evil tendencies within the person which will pass themselves on together with the good; in addition, the resulting social climate is no longer healthy, but rather orients one as much toward evil as toward good. "All have sinned," says the Apostle Paul, "and have been deprived of the glory of God" (Rom 3:25), of his holy presence, of an intimate relationship with him. For since this first choice, the root of sin is present in a man or woman from the day of birth, like a venom in the organs which are being formed within the child to be born from a pregnant woman who was supposed to have been bitten by a serpent. "For behold, in sin was I conceived and in evil was I brought forth by the labor of my mother" (Ps 51:7).

How can we uproot this sin which has been implanted in us, in every person, and within all of humanity? Paul explains further that this must be the work of God himself: "All have sinned, and are thus deprived of the glory of God, but have been freely justified by his grace, in virtue of the deliverance accomplished in Jesus Christ" (Rom 3:23-24). This sick and soiled humanity, this polluted and fallen humanity, God in his goodness has healed and purified, has transformed it and saved it in an absolutely free fashion through the intervention of his Son, Jesus Christ. The Savior acts like an antidote within each person condemned to death because of the fatal bite of the serpent.

But is this not also the work of humanity, for it is necessary that people freely confess Jesus as Lord and believe in his resurrection (cf. Rom 10:9)? This is true, in the sense that it is a matter here of the reception of a free gift; but this confession on the lips and this belief in the heart, to be given and embraced freely, are, in the first instance, God's initiative. "No one can say that Jesus is Lord unless he is guided by the Holy Spirit" (1 Cor 12:3); and what's more, it is God who vivifies those whose faith puts them in contact with God: "The just [that is, the one recognized by God as worthy] will live by faith" (Rom 1:17).

Because of this, the salvation won by Jesus can be compared to a plant. The fruit is available to anyone who wishes to gather it, to receive it in an act of faith: to confess it on the lips and to believe it in their heart. But its root lies in the infinite goodness of God alone, who gives (with regard to sin, who forgives) and who offers the world a unique gift in Jesus Christ, the Savior.

In the final analysis Paul connects the gift of faith with baptism. Inaugurated by faith, Christian existence begins with baptism. "By faith you have become sons and daughters of God in Jesus Christ. All you who have been baptized in Christ have put on Christ" (Gal 3:26-27). Paul explains it clearly: "By faith you have been united to Jesus Christ and become truly sons and daughters of God; for, if you have been baptized in Christ [that is, plunged into him, through him, with him, and like him], then, just as one replaces worn out clothes that hang from your skin with those that fits properly and which become one with you, you have now taken on his condition of perfect personhood that knows nothing of sin."

Paul is correct to link baptism to faith in this way. For faith implies an action: to confess on the lips and to believe in the heart; but it is also a gift from God: the support of the Holy Spirit is necessary for this act, and faith thus has its source in God. But that is exactly what baptism expresses (the word baptism means "immersed"). Water is there for the bath: to wash yourself, you have to get in. But the power of cleansing lies beyond: for something to rise up with the power to purify, the power of God is needed.

SUMMARY: *The Word of God, corroborated by human experience (this is the way God speaks) shows that humankind is a sinner and needs to be saved from this misery. The same Word of God states that God saves through Jesus Christ. The Word also adds that those baptized in Christ are saved in the very root of their being: all the more is it now necessary for them to freely respond by a profession of faith in this salvation to receive its fruits.*

JESUS AS SAVIOR

"I must receive this baptism," Jesus said, "and how it weighs upon me until this is accomplished" (Luke 12:50). Of what baptism is he speaking? Hasn't he already been baptized in the Jordan by John before beginning his ministry of healing and preaching?

In Mark's Gospel also it is a question for Jesus of this baptism that is coming. Two of his followers, James and John, approach him asking to be allowed ''to sit with him when he comes into his glory, one on his right and the other on his left:'' which means in effect, to become his highest ministers, not simply honored in that capacity but actually sharing in his power! And Jesus answers them: ''Can you drink from the cup that I will drink, or to be baptized with the baptism with which I will be baptized?'' (Mark 10:38), as if it were a question here of some sort of unavoidable test if one is to have access to the glory and the power that comes with such a position, for in the Old Testament, the cup is a symbol and figure for affliction and desolation (cf. Ezek 23:33).

This baptism that stands before Jesus is indeed the cup of suffering and of death. On three occasions he announces to those around him the passion he has to undergo: ''He began to teach them that the Son of Man must suffer much, be rejected by his own people, the high priests, and the scribes, that he be put to death, and that after three days he would rise from the dead'' (Mark 8:31; see also Luke 9:22, Matt 17:22). And a third time: ''Behold we are going up to Jerusalem; the Son of man will be delivered over to the high priests and the scribes: they will condemn him to death and will hand him over to unbelievers; They will mock him, spit on him; they will whip him, they will kill him and, after three days, he will rise'' (Mark 10:33-34; see also Luke 18:31; Matt 20:18).

It is worth noting that in these texts the prediction of the passion and death is followed by that of the resurrection (except in Luke 9:44, but it is doubtless to lay stress on the incomprehension of the disciples with regard to the passion that Luke there says nothing about the resurrection).

Thus, the passage of Jesus through suffering and death to reach the life of glory is indeed this testing baptism of which he speaks with James and John (Mark 10:38) and which he must undergo to carry out his mission as the Savior (Luke 12:49-50).

But has this baptism any consequences? Has it any effect?

Does it do anything? If the answer is yes, what *are* the fruits of this immersion of Jesus in death?

The consequences and the fruits of the baptism of Jesus into death are immense: it removes the sin of the world. For in fact, before going to the Jordan to be baptized, Jesus heard himself referred to in this speech of John who was baptizing, the last and perhaps the greatest of the prophets of the Old Law: ''Behold the Lamb of God, who takes away the sin of the world'' (John 1:29).

The Lamb of God, the lamb without blemish, is the victim offered and consumed in Israel at the moment of Passover:

> Let each family take one animal. . . The entire tribe of Israel will fill themselves at dusk. Take the blood; smear it on the two doorposts and the lintel of the houses where you are eating this meal. . . . The blood will serve as a sign for the houses where you are. I shall see the blood. I shall pass over you, and the destructive scourge will not touch you when I strike the land of Egypt (Exod 12:1-14).

Protected by the blood of the sacrificial lamb, the people of God escape the punishment inflicted upon their Egyptian masters who kept them in bondage.

The one who takes away the sin of the world is the expiating victim whom the prophet Isaiah presents in his fourth Servant Song:

> Man of sorrows . . . it is our sufferings that he carried, it is our sorrows that he supported, we considered him cursed, struck down by God and humiliated. But the Lord caused our perversity to fall upon him. Beaten, he humbled himself, he opened not his mouth, like a lamb led to the slaughter (Isa 53:3-8).

The innocent victim carried the sin of others to the point of removing it from them.

The immersion of Jesus in his passion, his baptism into death, makes him ''the lamb of God who takes away the sin of the world'' fulfilling the oracle of Isaiah and the prophecy of John the Baptist: at the time of Noah, the sinners were inundated and covered by the rising waters; at the time of Moses and of Pharaoh, the persecutors (those who harassed the Israelites) were swamped in the waters of the sea; in his own time, Jesus was entombed in death. It is a similar work of purification in each case, with the difference that the contemporaries of Noah and the Egyptians were punished as malefactors or as oppressors, while Jesus as the innocent victim undergoes his torture and his death as our replacement. He who did not know sin, God made sin for us, so that through him we might become the the justice of God (2 Cor 5:21). In truth, Jesus was without sin, but God weighed him down with our sin to purify us and to permit us, we sinners, to enter into intimacy with himself.

But the baptism of Jesus into death is at the same time his entrance into the life of God. This is what Peter proclaims to the Jews on the feast of Pentecost: "You delivered him over and suppressed him by crucifying him through the hands of unbelievers, but God raised him up in delivering him from the sorrows of death, for it was not possible for death to keep him in its power" (Acts 2:23-24). Peter further quotes David to support him: "For you will not abandon my life on the day of death and you will not allow your holy one to know dissolution" (Ps 16:10). Jesus, the holy one, having never committed a sin, undergoes death. But it was not possible that he be engulfed by it: much to the contrary, he triumphs over it through the resurrection. "Risen from the dead, Christ dies no more; death has no more power over him. For in dying, he has died to sin one time for all; living, he lives to God" (Rom 6:9-10). Jesus, dead through his solidarity with the human race whose condition he came to share, but raised up because he was without sin, lives from now on the life of God.

Baptized into death and resurrection, having thus rejoined the very life of God, Jesus passes on the benefits to us: "Just as the fall of one man led to the condemnation of all," Paul writes, "so the just act of one is the justification of all that gives life" (Rom 5:18). And it is by baptism, St. Paul explains further, that we benefit from this justification: "All of us, baptized into Jesus Christ, have been baptized into his death. By being baptized into his death, we have been entombed with him so that, just as Christ was raised up from the dead by the glory of the Father, so also we may lead a new life. For if we have been totally unified, assimilated into his death, we shall also be into his resurrection. . . . Reflect that you are dead to sin and alive to God in Jesus Christ (Rom 6:3-5, 11). Thus, through baptism, we have been buried with him to become dead with him, so as to be raised up with him to live through his life. All this is what is accomplished through the baptism in blood of Jesus.

SUMMARY: *The baptism of Jesus in his own blood on the cross takes away the sin of the world and transfers humanity from death to life. For the Christian, baptism means taking the same route from death to sin to resurrection in this new life.*

JESUS BAPTIZED

Before Jesus came to know the baptism in blood on the cross, baptism in water was a ritual practiced in Israel: at the moment when Jesus began his ministry of healing and preaching, the prophet John the Baptist, of whom the evangelist Mark speaks from the beginning of his account, called out immediately to him: "John the Baptist appeared in the desert, proclaiming a baptism of conversion for the forgiveness of sins. The entire land of Judea and all the inhabitants of Jerusalem came out to him: they had themselves baptized by him in the Jordan while confessing their sins" (Mark 1:4-5).

John the Baptist announced in these terms the arrival of another prophet much more important than himself: "I have baptized you with water, but he will baptize you with the Holy Spirit" (Mark 1:8).

But behold, this Jesus, this prophet announced in advance as baptizing in the Holy Spirit, he who was God made man, perfectly holy, without sin, comes forward in the midst of the crowd to be baptized like an ordinary sinner! One can understand the surprise and the reticence of John the Baptist: "It

is I who should be baptized by you, and yet you come to me''
(Mark 3:14).

What is the meaning and the significance of this baptism of
Jesus by John?

''Let it go ahead for now: it is fitting that in this way all justice be carried out'' (Matt 3:15) replies Jesus. This statement
deserves a closer study. In considering carefully each of the
words in this answer, especially in the Greek text, one grasps
the sense better, which goes: ''Do not decline this moment:
for behold, for us two (you who baptize and I who am going
to have myself baptized), this is the precise means by which
we shall render fully effective the settlement in accord with
justice (the justice of God); the quittance of this unjust debt
that God does not recognize.'' In this way the baptism of Jesus
in the waters of the Jordan opens new perspectives and gives
to the baptism which John administers to him much larger
dimensions: it announces the baptism in the Holy Spirit and
anticipates Jesus's bloody baptism.

Even in John's eyes, the baptism of conversion for the forgiveness of sins appeared insufficient: ''One who is stronger
than I comes after me. . . . I have baptized you with water,
but he will baptize you with the Holy Spirit'' (Mark 1:7-8; see
also Matt 3:11; Luke 3:16). After Jesus had himself begun to
baptize some time after his own baptism, when John was asked
about this, he responded: ''He must increase, and I must de-
crease'' (John 3:30). Jesus will not totally suppress the baptism
of John, but he will eclipse it, just as the full sun eclipses the
light of a candelabra: not only does the baptism of Jesus have
the effect of stripping away personal sin as one would pull
down a clinging vine from a tree; the baptism of Jesus does
much more: it cuts the parasitical growth off at its base, ''it
takes away the sin of the world''; it uproots sin.

For Jesus is the first to be baptized with a baptism where the
Holy Spirit reveals himself. Doubtless John performed the same
gestures and said the same words over him as he said over
others, but Mark writes that God manifested himself by tear-
ing open the heavens at the moment when Jesus came up out
of the water (1:10). John the Baptist gives witness to it when
he says: ''I saw the Spirit in the form of a dove descend from

heaven and remain over him. I did not know him, but he who sent me to baptize with water, it was he who said to me: He on whom you will see the Spirit come down and rest; it is he who will baptize in the Holy Spirit'' (Mark 1:11); ''This is my beloved Son, he whom it has pleased me to choose'' (Matt 3:17). At the baptism of Jesus, the Father, the Son, and the Spirit are present: the Father affirms there his will that ''all mankind be saved'' (1 Tim 2:4), the Son receives there his mission as Savior, and the Spirit there confers on him his anointing as Savior.

It is at his baptism, in fact, that Jesus is consecrated Messiah. The Father's voice there pronounces, in words taken from Psalm 2, words which recognize him as the Messiah: ''You are my Son, today I have begotten you'' (Luke 2:22). This is the affirmation of his divinity: this Jesus baptized in the Jordan is indeed ''this shoot sprung from the root of Jesse on whom rests the Spirit of the Lord, the spirit of wisdom and of discernment, the spirit of counsel and of courage, the spirit of knowledge and of fear of the Lord'' (Isa 11:1-2). Such is the declaration officially proclaimed from the height of the heavens: Jesus is the Messiah, he is the Christ, ''he who has been anointed.''

This anointing also bestows on him his mission. The Apostle Peter recalls it in his speech when he is sent by the Spirit to baptize Cornelius, the Roman officer, the first non-Jew to be baptized both with the Spirit and with water: this Jesus, he says, ''started in Galilee, after the baptism proclaimed by John; this Jesus came from Nazareth, you know well how God conferred upon him the oil of the Holy Spirit and of power; he went everywhere doing good; he cured all whom the devil kept in bondage, for God was with him'' (Acts 10:38).

This baptism of Jesus where the Holy Spirit manifests himself is a veritable anticipation of his baptism in blood on the cross. For Jesus there provides the true significance of the gesture of his humiliation on calvary and of his recovery by the Father on the day of his resurrection. ''He was pushed down, becoming obedient even unto death, death on a cross. That is why God raised him up to majesty. . . .'' (Phil 2:8-9). It is there that he becomes, as a hope for humanity but really, like a seed containing the entire plant, "the lamb of God who takes away the sin of the world," as John the Baptist designates him in the present: "Behold. . . ." (John 1:29).

Jesus is thus already armed for combat as the expiatory victim called to remove not only the personal sins for which the Jews presented themselves for John's baptism but also the poisonous seed and infected root of sin. At the instigation of the Spirit, this combat begins immediately: "Right away the Spirit led Jesus into the desert. For forty days in the desert he was tempted by Satan" (Mark 1:12-13; see also Matt 4:1; Luke 4:1). "Thus the devil is unchained, but from now on he is conquered; he knows he will soon be stripped, exposed in public, and dragged behind the triumphant procession of the cross" (Col 2:15). Victorious Roman military leaders led their defeated opponents as captives in the cortege behind them in their victory parades; this is the way, for example, Julius Caesar treated Vercingetorix. In the same way Satan is now subjected to Jesus Christ for all eternity. Thus Jesus's baptism by water is the anticipation of his bloody baptism on the cross in the sense that it is the starting moment of his mission, the inaugural event of salvation.

But the inauguration is not yet the final harvest; the fine-tuning of an exposition is not yet its presentation to a larger public, nor is the dress rehearsal of a show the same thing as its opening night. And yet in another sense, it is all there, in that this is what will be happening or going on for the entire length of the exposition or as long as the show is running. Thus it is with the baptism of Jesus: there was only a short lapse of time, two or three years, between the incident at the Jordan and the event at Calvary, during which Jesus was saving; "Your sins are forgiven," he said to the paralyzed man at Capharnaum and to the public sinner who came to anoint his feet at the house of Simon (Mark 2:5; Luke 7:48). But salvation was extended to all only with Jesus's baptism into blood: "It pleased God to concentrate in him all his fullness and to reconcile all through him and for him, on the earth and in the heavens, having established peace by the blood of his cross" (Col 1:19-20).

One should appreciate not only the extent but also the depth of this salvation: both reach to the unimaginable limits of sin itself. Since the creation of the world, personal sins have been so numerous, so often repeated, and so grave that in the end they have given rise to what Pope John Paul II calls "sinful structures."[1] These, he writes, "are self-reinforcing, have an internal dynamism of expansion, and become thereby the source of still more sins; further, they condition the behavior of entire populations." It is a matter here "of a moral evil, resulting from multiple sins which taken cumulatively, become gradually taken for granted, and ultimately produce sinful structures."[2]

Against this, the victory of Jesus on the Cross, contained in its entirety *in nuce* in his baptism in the Jordan like a seed programmed to produce a certain fruit, strangles evil at that very point. You are amidst trials and persecutions, Jesus says; however, I am in the process of dominating every species of egoism, every unconscious mechanism and blind habit, as well as the desire for profit and thirst for power which are at their source: "In this world you are in distress, but take courage, for I have overcome the world" (John 16:33).

SUMMARY: *The baptism of Jesus in the Jordan announces the baptism of the Holy Spirit: those baptized will no longer come imploring the remission of their sins, but they will be assured of this and will receive the Holy Spirit. The baptism of Jesus also anticipates his baptism in blood: in sketching there the action of abasement and humiliation and of recovery he will execute really on the cross and during Easter night, he is already victorious in his mission through the Spirit.*

THE BAPTISM OF THE DISCIPLES

Jesus was baptized with water in the Jordan and with blood on the cross. But his baptism with water at the hands of John the Baptist was something quite different from a baptism of conversion for the remission of sins: rather, it was a baptism where the Holy Spirit became manifest, which signifies and anticipates the baptism in blood through which he is Savior of the world and triumphant over sin. But what kind of baptism did his disciples receive? A baptism in water? A baptism in the Holy Spirit? Both?

At least a few of them received the baptism of John the Baptist in the Jordan: John the Evangelist and Andrew were disciples of the Baptist at the time of their calling by Jesus (cf. John 1:35-40). Jesus himself, according to John 3:22, or rather his disciples according to John 4:2, began to baptize as well: it is thus probable that "those who came to him" received at that time a baptism in water. But as yet this could only have been a "baptism of conversion aiming at the remission of sins," a religious act whereby man seeks to raise himself up to God, while after Jesus's baptism in blood, it is God himself who reaches down to the sinner to save him. John's Gospel is quite firm on this point. On the last day of the feast of tabernacles, Jesus in fact says: "If anyone is thirsty, let him come to me, and let he who believes in me drink." As Scripture itself says (not in one specific passage, but by continually invoking the image of waters springing up): "from his side will flow streams of living water." "In this way he indicated the Spirit that those who believed in him would receive; but in fact, as yet the Spirit had not yet come, for Jesus had not yet been glorified" (John 7:37-40). In that Jesus had not yet been immersed in death and had not yet been led back from death to life through the resurrection, although he had already been consecrated by the Spirit for his mission, he does not yet baptize in the Holy Spirit and does not give to anyone the power to do so in his name.

He will give this power to the Twelve at the time of his going up to heaven, his ascension, at the moment of his last apparition among them; and with it his evangelical instructions: "All power has been given me in the heavens and on earth. Go then to make disciples of all nations, baptizing them in the name of the Father and the Son and the Holy Spirit. . . ." (Matt 28:18-19; see also Mark 16:15-16). John even writes that this evangelical instruction goes back to the evening of the resurrection and was accompanied by a sending of the Holy Spirit: " 'As the Father has sent me, so I send you.' Having spoken thus, he breathed on them and said to them: 'Receive the Holy Spirit. . . .' '" (John 20:21-22). It is a matter here of a breath that brings the dead to life and calls into existence what has not existed (Rom 4:17), that brings dead bones back to life (cf. Ezek 37:9), of the Spirit active at creation (cf. Gen 1:7). Is this not already a manifestation of baptism in the Holy Spirit?

Against this, according to Luke the event of Pentecost occurred several weeks later. Already on the eve of his Passion, Jesus had promised the Holy Spirit to the Twelve: "I shall ask the Father, and he will send you another Advocate who will remain with you always" (John 14:16), that is to say, an advocate who will defend you in the trial that the world will make against you. "The Paraclete, the Holy Spirit whom the Father will send you in my name, will teach you all things and will make you remember all that I have said" (John 14:26). One may also quote John 16:7-15. At the moment of the ascension, the reason for the coming of the Holy Spirit is also made clear: "You shall receive a power, that of the Holy Spirit who will come upon you; then you shall be my witnesses. . . ." (Acts 1:8). And behold! Like a hurricane, with noise, wind, and fire, Pentecost arrives with such extraordinary phenomena. Appearing intoxicated, but in reality elated, the Apostles express themselves in such a way that everyone, Jew and foreigner alike, understands them each in his own tongue, intimating thereby the universal dimension of the mission of the Church that is at that moment coming to birth (cf. Acts 2), a Church called to bring back together humankind that was scattered and dispersed at Babel (cf. Gen 11). This behavior was taken for drunkenness, but Peter explained immediately that it was rather the fulfillment of the prophecy of Joel: "In those days I shall spread out my Spirit, and they shall be prophets" (Acts 2:18). Is not the occurrence at Pentecost *par excellence* the "Baptism in the Holy Spirit"?

Other manifestations of the Spirit could be mentioned from the Book of Acts, such as that called the "Small Pentecost." Having proclaimed the resurrection from the dead, Peter and John are brought before the Jewish council (the Sanhedrin, which had condemned Jesus). They were set free, but the community was worried and began to pray fervently. "At the conclusion of their prayer, the place where they were located was lit up: they were all filled with the Holy Spirit and spoke with assurance the word of God'' (Acts 4:31). Further, as one continues reading Acts, one observes that the Apostles allow themselves to be led by the Spirit for the spread of the Gospel, the Good News of Salvation.

Following the Gospels and Acts, therefore, one can retrace the progress of the Twelve: they could have received baptism in water during the earthly life of Jesus, they received the Holy Spirit the evening of Easter (cf. John 20), they were baptized in the Holy Spirit on the day of Pentecost, and later often received a visit or the support of this same Spirit.

But what kind of baptism was administered in the early days by the disciples themselves or by other disciples of Christ? Was this still the baptism of John "for conversion and the remission of sins?" Was this a baptism in the name of Jesus? Or was this a baptism in the Holy Spirit?

A baptism of conversion for the remission of sins could have been practiced by disciples of John who also knew of the teachings of Jesus. Proof of this is the presence at Ephesus of the intellectual Jew Apollos, who "preached and taught correctly about Jesus but who only knew of the baptism of John" (Acts 18:24). When Paul arrives at Ephesus, Apollos is no longer there, but Paul finds there a dozen believers; however, the latter "had heard nothing of the Holy Spirit and had received only the baptism of John." Thus Paul teaches them: "John gave a baptism of conversion and asked the Jews to believe in he who would come after him, that is to say, in Jesus" (Acts 19:4). Paul then baptizes them "in the name of the Lord Jesus and imposed hands on them; and the Holy Spirit came upon them; they spoke in tongues and prophesied." This account thus distinguishes the baptism of John, a properly Christian baptism in the name of Jesus that is similarly a baptism in water, and the imposition of hands to which the appearance of the Spirit is evidently linked.

However, baptism in water in the name of Jesus and the imposition of hands with the appearance of the Holy Spirit can also be separated from one another by a certain lapse of time. During their mission in Samaria, Peter and John encountered some believers who "had received baptism in the name of the Lord Jesus"; it apparently consisted in baptism in water given in the same manner as John, but done now in the name of the Lord Jesus. This baptism establishes an intimate relation with the person of Jesus, because for the Jews a person and his name are one and the same thing. One cannot insist upon this point enough: the name of Jesus is his person. It was he who healed the sick man at the Temple at the instigation of Peter's prayer (cf. Acts 3:16). However, Peter and John, in the presence of these Samaritans who had been baptized in the name of Jesus, observe that the Spirit had nonetheless not appeared, that "the Spirit had not fallen upon any of them," that this baptism had thus not had any visible effect. That is why "they began to impose hands on them, and the Samaritans received the Holy Spirit" (Acts 8:18). Was this followed by indications of his presence? We must believe that it was, for if not (as the text continues), Simon the magician would not have envied the Apostles their power and asked them to teach it to him. Thus, these Samaritans first received a baptism in water in the name of Jesus which put them into relation with him, then later an imposition of hands whose effect (that is, an appearance of the Holy Spirit) did not escape Simon.

On the other hand, Cornelius and the first non-Jews who heard the Word of God about Jesus Christ received the Holy Spirit directly during Peter's preaching; it was immediately after this appearance of the Spirit among them that Peter felt himself moved to baptize his hearers who had been thus touched by the Spirit:

> Peter was explaining these matters when the Holy Spirit fell upon all those who had heard the Word. This caused amazement among the believers who had been circumcized who had accompanied Peter; the gift of the Spirit was now extended even to the pagan nations! For in fact they heard these people speaking in tongues and praising the greatness of God. Then Peter began to speak: "Could anyone forbid us to baptize with water these people who, like us, have received the Holy Spirit?" He gave the command to baptize them in the name of Jesus Christ, and they asked him to remain among them several days more (Acts 10:44-48).

We are thus confronted with an appearance of the Holy Spirit which takes place exclusively on the divine initiative, before any baptism in water and dispensing with the imposition of hands. That recalls the incident where Paul is struck down while on the road to Damascus, converted by a direct call from God but baptized later by Ananias (cf. Acts 9:18). The freedom of the Spirit is indeed boundless, which normally operates following baptism in water and the prayer of believers, but which may also operate, as here, without this baptism, or at least before it. However, one should mention that Cornelius was one of the ''God fearers,'' that is to say, a non-Jew who was not circumcized but who nevertheless worshiped the God of the Jews and desired to know him. It was on the basis of a vision (cf. Acts 10:1-9) that he sent men to look for Peter at Joppa and expected his visit. From this event may one not conclude that he had an implicit if unconscious desire for baptism? The theologians of the Middle Ages, considering this wish to be saved together with the will of God to save all people (cf. 1 Tim 2:6), concluded that this desire would have the same effect as baptism.

It is still true that the situation is that of a call to baptism in the name of Jesus. Peter encourages this at the conclusion of his first discourse, linking the gift of the Holy Spirit with baptism in the name of Jesus: ''Be converted: let each of you receive baptism in the name of Jesus Christ for the forgiveness of your sins, and you will receive the gift of the Holy Spirit'' (Acts 2:38). This is exactly what happened when Philip baptized the treasurer of the queen of Ethiopia on the road leading from Jerusalem to Gaza. Philip, after having instructed him, baptized him. ''When they came up out of the water, the Spirit of the Lord carried Philip away, and the eunuch [the queen's treasurer] saw him no more, but he continued on his way in joy'' (Acts 8:39). There is no question here of prophecies, nor of speaking in tongues, nor of frenzy, but of the joy which is a fruit of the Spirit (cf. Gal 5:22).

So Christian baptism is entirely different from the baptism of John. Of course, it presupposes on the part of those who have been touched by the Word a similar human response in respect of the remission of sins, but it is entirely from God:

it is given in the name of Jesus, that is to say, the Savior dead and raised up who alone has the power to pardon sins. As for the gift of the Spirit, no doubt it is linked to this baptism, just as Peter promised (Acts 2:38) and the case of the eunuch illustrates. All our other texts connect the appearance of the Spirit with the imposition of hands: the only exception is the baptism of Cornelius, but there it is a case of a divine initiative in response to the profound desire of Cornelius. Thus these exterior manifestations (or interior, like joy) appear as the fruits of this seed that is the baptism in blood of Jesus. And baptism in water is the sign and application to each Christian of this baptism of Jesus into his death and resurrection.

SUMMARY: *The Apostles received the Holy Spirit the evening after the resurrection, but the visible manifestation of this same Spirit only took place later with the renewal of this gift on the day of Pentecost. Those first to be baptized were baptized in the name of Jesus in accordance with his fairwell command: "Go . . . baptize them in the name of the Father, of the Son, and of the Holy Spirit." This is what gives them the divine life, otherwise expressed, the spiritual life, or life in the Spirit. The latter appeared immediately after, as in the interior joy of the Ethiopian eunuch, but also before, as with Cornelius and his companions. It appeared after the imposition of hands which follows baptism, whether the latter was carried out immediately after baptism as at Ephesus, or a little later as at Samaria.*

THOSE BORN ANEW

So once it has occurred, what does baptism change? In his letters to the various Christian communities, the Apostle Paul frequently takes up the topic of baptism: he teaches that the baptized person now finds himself in an intimate relation with Jesus, lives from now on by his Spirit, has become a child of God, is born anew, and is a member of his body.

The thrust of Paul's teaching on this topic concerns the sharing of the baptized person in Jesus' baptism in blood: through their baptism, Christians have themselves also gone through a death and resurrection, from death to sin to life in God. "By our baptism into his death, we have been buried with him, so that, as Christ was raised from the dead by the glory of the Father, we also might lead a new life. For if we have been totally united and assimilated to his death, so shall we also be to his resurrection" (Rom 6:4-5). Paul insists upon putting this immersion into the death and resurrection of Christ into connection with faith: "Buried with him in baptism, you have also been raised up with him, because you have believed in the power of God who raised him from the dead" (Col 2:12).

Elsewhere Paul uses the image of clothing: "Yes, all you who have been baptized in Christ, you have put on Christ. . . . You all are one in Jesus Christ" (Gal 3:26, 28). This is, however, not a matter of a simple change of externals; it is rather the very being of the baptized person which is transformed: "You have taken off the old man with his habits and you have put on the new man" (Col 3:9-10) or more simply: "If anyone is in Christ, he is a new creation" (2 Cor 5:17). It is the very meaning of Christian life to be a communion in the divine life of Christ. This is what Paul stresses: "With Christ I am crucified; I live, but it is no longer I, it is Christ who lives in me. For I view my present life in the flesh through faith in the son of God" (Gal 2:19-20).

Paul thus insists upon this realism: it is a process of vital assimilation to Christ. The Most Alive One *par excellence* assimilates those baptized the way a living being assimilates nutrition. Here however it is a process of spiritual assimilation, of our life into the Spirit: "We have all been baptized into a single Spirit in a single body . . . and we have all been watered from a single Spirit" (1 Cor 12:13). On the relation of baptism to the Spirit, undoubtedly the clearest text is that of Titus: God has saved us "in virtue of his mercy through the bath of the new birth and of the renewal which the Holy Spirit produces" (Titus 3:5). Paul returns frequently to this theme of the spiritual presence of Christ in the Christian. To the wayward in Corinth he writes: "Do you not know that your body is the temple of the Holy Spirit who is in you?'' (1 Cor 6:19). His thought is clear: ''The Spirit of God lives in you. If someone does not have the Spirit of Christ, he does not belong to him'' (Rom 8:9).

But how does the Spirit of Christ reside in us? To understand this, one must recall the Bible's view of human reality: ''The Lord God formed man with dust taken from the earth. He blew into his nostrils the breath of life, and man became a living being'' (Gen 2:7). This imaginative description expresses what man is: a composite of clay from the earth and of breath. Thus man has an animal body but also a human spirit. However, Paul never loses sight of the fact that, due to sin, all of human life has been vitiated: ''It is sin that lives in me. . . . Who will free me from this body of death?'' (Rom 7:20-24). Who will free me from the sin because of which I must die, to live instead in Jesus Christ, transformed by the Spirit? For, without the Holy Spirit, one leads a human life that Paul describes by the term ''psychic,'' because a person possesses faculties of knowing and loving which the animals do not have, but also ''carnal'' (not to be confused with ''bodily'') because this psychic life has been infected with sin. On the other hand, with the Holy Spirit a person now leads a spiritual life; one's carnal life has been changed. Of course, since he is gifted with freedom, a Christian may act again as a carnal person, like the Corinthian who ''lived with his father's wife'' (1 Cor 5:1), something even civil law condemned. That does not alter the fact that one's psychic life that was carnal before baptism has become spiritual with the arrival of the Holy Spirit: in him, the spiritual has been substituted for the carnal.

Thus the Christian has entered into the intimacy of God, whom he or she may now call ''Father, Abba'' through the presence of the Spirit: ''This Spirit himself gives evidence to our spirit that we are children of God'' (Rom 8:16). The Holy Spirit whispers to our human spirit that he transforms what is carnal into the spiritual, and that we are now members of ''the family of God'' (Eph 2:20).

At the same time Paul describes us as adopted sons (v. 15), while John mentions our ''ability to become children of God'' (John 1:12), speaks of our ''new birth'' (John 3), and writes:

"See with what a great love the Father has gifted us, that we are called children of God; and we are. . . ." (1 John 3:1). Yes, we are, and this is beyond our wildest imagination: "Whoever is born of God sins no more" (1 John 5:18), "he can no longer sin because he is born of God" (1 John 3:9) on the condition, of course, of continuing to "walk in the light" without turning back toward the shadows (1 John 1:1-10): the Apostle John makes the same reservation as Paul, thereby distinguishing our permanent state as children of God, a new creation, and the follies which are always a possibility because of our freedom, and which God respects.

The vital assimilation of each one of us to the same Christ makes the baptized into members of a single Body of Christ; "We have all been baptized into a single Spirit, into a single body. . . ." (1 Cor 12:13); "There is only one body and one Spirit. . . one sole Lord, one sole faith, a single baptism" (Eph 4:4). This Body of Christ is thus the collection of the baptized called to holiness: "Christ has loved the Church and delivered himself up for her; he thus wished to render her holy by purifying her with the water that cleanses, and that through the Word" (Eph 5:25). It is indeed baptism that is being discussed; Christ has given his life for the Church to render her worthy of God, after having purified her through water and the Word, in short, through baptism. Each Christian is thus consecrated, "marked with the seal of the Spirit" (2 Cor 1:21; Eph 1:13).

SUMMARY: *Baptized into the death and resurrection of Christ, the Christian lives from the very life of God, a life according to the Spirit: a person's very being is profoundly affected by this; he or she passes through a new birth which transforms him or her into a child of God, a member of the Body of Christ, that is to say, of the Church which Jesus calls together and sanctifies through his Spirit.*

MORE THAN ONE BAPTISM?

The Letter to the Hebrews elevates to the status of fundamental principles . . . the doctrine of baptism and the imposition of hands (Heb 6:1). And as a matter of fact, the passages from the Gospels and the Acts of the Apostles quoted in the previous sections do permit us to distinguish:

The baptism by immersion given by John the Baptist in the Jordan (cf. Mark 1:4) and which was received by the twelve disciples whom Paul encountered at Ephesus (cf. Acts 19:4). This is a penitential devotion.

The baptism "in the name of Jesus," preached and administered by Peter after the event of Pentecost (Acts 2:38-41), which the converts in Samaria received (8:36), the Ethiopian eunuch after having heard "the good new thing" from the mouth of Philip (8:35-39), Paul himself (9:18), as also Cornelius (10:47-48) and also the twelve disciples from Ephesus already baptized by John (19:5). It is this baptism that the Churches today recognize as a sacrament.

The appearances of the Holy Spirit announced at the ascension (Acts 1:5 and 8) and fulfilled at Pentecost (Acts 2), renewed at the "small Pentecost" (4:30) and which the converts from Samaria experienced (8:17), the Apostle Paul (9:17), Cornelius (10:44) and some disciples of John at Ephesus (19:17). Following upon (although not always) the imposition of hands, this is recognized as the baptism in the Holy Spirit.

Finally, baptism by blood, announced to the sons of Zebedee (Mark 10:38), that of Jesus himself, and of so many martyrs who followed him who chose to die rather than to renounce him.

But the baptism where Christ builds up his Body through the Spirit is unique: "There is one sole body and one sole Spirit . . . one Lord only, one faith only, and only one baptism" (Eph 4:4-5).

CHAPTER TWO

The Practice of the Churches

WHY ARE THERE MANY CHURCHES?

The very first disciples of Jesus were Jews like himself. But, beginning with the preaching of the apostles, pagans started becoming Christians. There thus developed distinct Judeo-Christian and Gentile-Christian communities. At the same time the exclusively Judeo-Christian communities, at least the Church of Jerusalem, disappeared with the destruction of Jerusalem in A.D. 70.

Starting from this moment, in the East there developed communities where one spoke Greek, and others in the West where soon one spoke Latin. This was the time of the "undivided Church" which hammered out its faith through the first seven ecumenical councils down to the eighth century. There were indeed various separations which, starting with the fifth century and for doctrinal reasons (on the subject of Christ) gave rise to independent national Churches which persist to this day: the Coptic Church in Egypt, the Jacobite Church (from the name of its founder Jacob Baradaï) in Syria, and the Nestorian Churches (who believe, following Nestorius, that there exist two persons in Jesus Christ). However, these did not produce disastrous results like the great fractures of the second millennium.

The first of these fractures occurred in the eleventh century. To tell the truth, this fire had been smoldering for two centuries due to rivalries between the Eastern empire and the Western empire which had an impact on the life of the Churches:

to different doctrinal approaches were added an opposition between the centralization in Rome and the pretentions to prestige and independence by the patriarchs. A fatal development occurred in 1054 when Cardinal Humbert, the papal legate, excommunicated the Patriarch Michel Cerularius, who immediately reciprocated. Since that time there has been an Orthodox Church in the East formed by patriarchates and a Catholic Church in the West united around the bishop of Rome, the pope. Each has continued to live with its own language and its traditions, attire, and disciplines. Over the centuries they have become more and more differentiated from each other. True, an accord was worked out at the Council of Florence in 1439 by representatives of the two Churches, but this has remained without effect. It took until 1965 for the mutual excommunications to be lifted by Paul VI and Athenagoras I. At the present time the work of a joint Orthodox-Catholic commission is well advanced, but full communion between the two Churches is not yet a reality.

However, the Western Catholic Church, which had produced, like the Eastern Orthodox Church, so many fruits of holiness, found itself in the sixteenth century in such a lamentable condition that there arose reformers, who, unfortunately, were not successful at reforming the Church from within, but rather found themselves excluded. This is the source of the Protestant Churches, with Luther (called to a hearing in 1517 and condemned in 1520) and Calvin his younger follower. At the same time the king of England, Henry VIII formed a national Anglican Church separated from Rome.

Between the Catholic Church and the Protestant Churches, even before the Council of Trent opened in 1545 and the death of Luther, the doctrinal divergences were large. One fundamental difference in particular, which persists to this day, concerns the very nature of the Church.

For the Protestants there exist two levels to the Church: that of the Universal Church, and that of local Churches:

The Universal Church is the Body of Christ, invisible, whose members are known to God alone and that crosses all confessional lines, Lutheran, Calvinist, or any other, as well as all denominations.

The local Churches are the communities to which one belongs by birth or through a personal assimilation, which offer their members the possibility of worship by the proclamation of the Word, the sacraments of baptism and the Lord's Supper, and fraternal communion organized or not into groups, by biblical sharing, and other groups, with services of various sorts.

For Catholics united to Rome, there also exist two levels, but these are indissolubly linked:

The Church of Jesus Christ is, as for the Protestants, the Body of Christ, invisible, whose members are known to God alone. This Church certainly includes non-Catholics; (however, it is not always called "universal," for in Catholic circles this expression more often designates the collection of local Catholic Churches). But above all, in contrast to Protestants, this Church, the Spouse and the Body of Christ, is rooted in humanity just as the Son of God who has become man in Jesus Christ: it includes an institution, recognized as divine, joined through the ministry for the sanctification of the faithful, of which Christ is the minister through the Holy Spirit.

The local Church is the one which is assembled around the bishop and which, in its role as instrument associated with Christ, confers the sacraments, proclaims the Word, and brings to life fraternal communion in such a way that the entire Church of Jesus Christ is present in every local Church. That pertains to its structure indissolubly linked to the Church of Jesus Christ whose Spouse she is and over which he reigns in a way that crosses every difference. Currently—but this reflects a mode of organization which can change—the bishop is at the head of a diocese (always a territorial division), and the communities, parochial or otherwise, are divisions within the diocese.

From its beginning down to our own time, the reform of Luther and Calvin has given birth to many Churches; further, one notices today that these Churches have given rise to others, culminating with the appearance of many "denominations." Without tracing back the entire line of this generation, here are two examples which will be useful in the chapters that follow: the origin of the Baptists and that of the Pentecostals.

From the time even of Luther, certain Protestants, considered by all (Catholics and Protestants alike) as extremists, wished to live in complete fidelity to the Word, in particular in baptizing only those believers who were capable of personally professing their faith: these were the Anabaptists. The Catholic priest Menno converted to their doctrine and organized a Mennonite Church. In the following century some dissident English Calvinists took refuge in Holland. Impressed by the evangelical ideal of the Mennonites, on their return to England they gave birth to the Baptist Churches.

In the eighteenth century the Anglican priests John and Charles Wesley wished to quicken the pulse of their Church: in particular, they sought to stimulate its spiritual life through an "order of life" (in Latin, a "*methodus vitae*"): they separated into the Methodist Church. Repeating this process, at the very beginning of the twentieth century, an American Methodist preacher, Charles Fox Parham, having come to the conviction that the gift of tongues was the infallible biblical sign of an authentic "baptism in the Holy Spirit," started the Pentecostal Churches.

SUMMARY: *Today there are several large Churches and numerous Protestant denominations (some refer to themselves as "evangelical"). For, even though all of them confess Jesus Christ as Savior, they have different doctrines and practices: they do not all administer baptism in the same way, and each justifies their manner of doing so.*

A SOLEMN BAPTISM AROUND THE YEAR 500

Before we look at baptism in a few of the Churches today, it would no doubt be interesting to see how baptism was practiced in a time when the Church was still undivided. Formerly, while there were certainly different traditions, customs, and disciplines, all the Churches still professed the same faith, constantly affirmed, and made continually more precise by ecumenical councils.

In the sixth century, just after the first separations by several Eastern Churches, the Church already had a great abundance of rites (that is the texts for and the rules regulating ceremonies), but these did not take place in exactly the same way at Rome, tor example, as they did in Jerusalem or in France. Otherwise expressed, these rituals had already evolved differently, and would keep on doing so.

At Rome at the beginning of the sixth century there were many catechumens. A catechumen, according to the etymology of this word, is "someone who receives something which rings in his ears." One thus calls a candidate for baptism a "catechumen," for he or she must be instructed in the truths of the faith and come to understand them. The candidates for baptism at this period could remain in this status for many years: they had been received into the Church and were already considered members of the community. Together at the back of the basilica, they attended the first part of the Mass, made up principally of several readings of the Word; but they left at the moment when the celebration of the Eucharist began, that is, just after the proclamation of the gospel.

On feasts in general and at Easter in particular, a certain number of them would be baptized; from the first preparatory meeting on, they are no longer called catechumens, but the "elect."

On the Wednesday of the third week of Lent (Lent consists of the six weeks leading up to Easter), the elect who are going to be baptized at the Easter vigil were gathered at the Church of St. Mark or some other church by the clergy, priests, deacons, and exorcists, with their godfathers and godmothers and the community (the assembly of all the faithful, that is to say, those who profess the faith) to undergo a scrutiny. It consisted in verifying the aptitude of the candidate to live the Christian life, and this examination was the test which permitted one to be elected. This preparatory meeting had its own prayers and rituals. On the invitation of the deacon, each candidate was blessed by their godfather or godmother, who signed them "in the name of the Father and of the Son and of the Holy Spirit." After that an exorcist pronounced these words, among others, over the group: "Execrable Demon, acknowledge your condemnation: render homage to the true God, the Living

One, to Jesus Christ his Son and to the Holy Spirit; and depart from these servants of God." Then a priest imposed hands on them and offered a prayer of purification and sanctification. One then began the first part of the Mass with the newly elect, who, however, left when the Eucharist proper started.

Six other scrutinies followed during Lent, imposing a rigorous training for spiritual combat to be completed before baptism. Two of these scrutinies are especially important.

The fourth scrutiny, for which one met at St. Lawrence-outside-the- Walls, had for its object to pass on to the elect the disclosure of the truths that must be believed, for at this period there was practiced in the Church (and more strictly at Jerusalem than at Rome) the discipline of the Mysteries, only the baptized should know the mysteries of the faith, which are those truths which surpass human intelligence and which could only be revealed by God, who proposes them for acceptance by men. After songs and readings, during which the verse of Isaiah was proclaimed: "O You who are thirsty, come to the waters. . . ." (Isa 55), one reads the "Symbol of the Apostles" (or Apostles' Creed), the short "I believe in God" well known in our Churches, which the elect now hear for the first time. It is a "symbol" (in the sense of "manifestation" or "exteriorization") of the teachings of Jesus that is so old that St. Ambrose, the bishop of Milan, in the fourth century described it as "apostolic." This "Symbol of the Apostles" affirms a faith in God as creator, in Jesus Christ as Redeemer, in the Spirit as Sanctifier, in the Church and eternal life. It moves from the creation of the world to the ultimate destiny of humanity. That is why, during this scrutiny, each part of it was explained at length.

The Elect then received the text of the Our Father in the same way.

The seventh scrutiny completed this gradual initiation on the Saturday morning before Easter (Holy Saturday) at the Lateran Basilica. The bishop comes and begins by tracing the Sign of the Cross on the foreheads of each of the elect, then pronounces an exorcism over the entire group before repeating over each the gesture Jesus made while curing the deaf-and-dumb man: "Be thou opened" (Mark 7:34). The bishop then questions each one of the elect three times: "Do you renounce Satan? . . . And his pomps? . . . And his works?"—"I do." Satan's pomps are the pagan spectacles and blandishments by which the demon insinuated himself craftily with deceit, sacrifices to idols, augery, etc., and also gladiatorial combats, games in the circus for which the masses were enthusiastic—in short, the "world" in the sense John uses it in his Gospel. There follows a ritual of anointing: with oil blessed on the preceding Thursday (Holy Thursday), the bishop traces the Sign of the Cross between the shoulders and on the exposed chest of the elect. This signifies that the latter, freed from Satan, will now have to compete as athletes in the faith. The ceremony concludes with the most important: having learned and considered, assimilated, and accepted the Apostles' Creed, each of them ascends to the ambo, the stone podium situated in the nave, to proclaim their faith by reciting this creed: it is not sufficient to believe it privately, one must be ready to affirm it publically. "If you confess with your mouth . . . and if you believe in your heart, says the Word of God" (Rom 10:9).

The Vigil of Easter has arrived: the assembly is collected in the nave, the elect remain at the back of the basilica, men on one side, women on the other, everyone in darkness; the bishop and his clergy ascend the nave in procession to take their places in the apse where the episcopal throne is located: they are led by an enormous candle which throws the only light there is in the whole church, and the people begin already to chant the joy of the resurrection. However, at the period of which we are speaking, the ritual of blessing the candle was not yet practiced at Rome, and the canticle of joy *Exultet jam angelica turba coelorum.* . . . "Let the choirs of angels in heaven rejoice!" had not yet been composed. There then followed a long reading of a dozen scriptural passages interspersed with prayers of supplication. In this way one recounted the events of creation, the flood, the sacrifice of Abraham, the crossing of the Red Sea, the prophecies of Isaiah, of Baruch, Ezechiel's vision of dry bones, etc. It is a vigil, a watch; one looks back, and one looks forward to the resurrection.

The moment of baptism has come: the procession forms to

move toward the baptistry, where the elect take their places with their godparents, to the intonations of Psalm 42: "As a deer longs for flowing waters, so my soul yearns for you, my God. I thirst for God, the living God: When may I enter and see the face of God." At the Church of the Lateran, the baptistry is large enough for two pools, one on each side (one served for the immersion of the men, the other for women) fed by a spring in the center and emptied by a drain. On this occasion the walls are decorated with white hangings and the air is thick with incense. Upon entering, the bishop invokes the Spirit with a formula for the solemn blessing of the water: *Descendat in hanc plenitudinem fontis virtus Spiritus Sancti . . .* "May the power of the Holy Spirit descend even to the bottom of this pool."

Approximately two centuries later, one finds traces of two rites signifying the union of the Spirit with the water: in the one, the bishop breathes on the water, and in the other he mixes chrism (a mixture of oil and balsm) in it. Were perhaps one or the other of these rites already in use at Rome at the beginning of the sixth century? Whatever the case, the water which cleanses the body is called on to signify and achieve the purification of the entire human being.

Everything is now ready for the baptism. The elect are completely stripped of their clothing (as was the custom then at public baths). The first one goes down into the pool, above which one may read the inscription, among others: "Behold the Lamb of God, who takes away the sin of the world"; the bishop interrogates him: "Have you renounced Satan? . . . Have you attached yourself to Christ?"; he then immerses him three times saying: "I baptize you in the name of the Father, and of the Son, and of the Holy Spirit." The bishop baptizes several more in the same manner and the priests continue, while the deaconesses baptize the women in the adjoining room where there is also a pool. The elect who has become a neophyte (in English, a "new born") climbs up from the pool to receive oil made with chrism from the priest, and a white tunic and coat from his godfather, after he has welcomed and dried him.

The last ritual is the anointing with chrism. After having baptized the first of the elect, the bishop moves to a nearby room, the chapel of consignment. It is there that he will receive the neophytes in groups, to impose hands upon them while calling upon the Spirit for the Seven Gifts (cf. Isa 11:2) and to anoint them with holy chrism to render them sharers in the royal priesthood of Jesus Christ—Priest, Prophet, and King. This unction, reserved to the bishop, is like a seal which marks the completion of the immersion into the death and resurrection of the Anointed One: the Christian now lives proudly like, with, and through Jesus Christ, resurrected and living.

CATHOLICS

The rites of the Catholic Church stand in direct line with the customs just described: some differences come from an attempt to update them. Today there exist three rites (or rituals) for baptism: one for the baptism of adults, another for that of infants, and a third, which is new, for children of a school age.

Each of these three rituals requires the same general preliminaries, where one can read: "it is through baptism that humankind, becoming a single body in Christ, forms the people of God. After having received forgiveness for all their sins and after having been "rescued from the power of darkness," they are "transported from" the human condition in which they were born, to the status of "children by adoption" (Col 1:13; Rom 8:15; Gal 4:5): their birth by water and the Holy Spirit makes of them a new creation. It is thus that they are called "children of God," which they now truly are (1 John 3:1). The participation through baptism in the death and resurrection of Christ is also clearly stated: "Those who are baptized, become one with Christ through a death like his . . . buried with him in death" (Rom 6:5-4), they are also "brought back to life in him and raised up with him" (Eph 2:5-6). For baptism is nothing other than the remembrance of the mystery of Easter which is effective insofar as it leads humans from the death of sin to life."

The baptismal ritual for adults plots a steady advance in faith toward baptism and even beyond, and suggests four stages to this journey, each one culminating in a celebration.

The first stage occurs before formal entry into the catechumenate: it is the period between the request for baptism, whose motivation must be examined, and a first celebration. It is the time of an initial instruction whose goal is the beginning of faith and a first conversion, as well as the first contacts with the Church. A Christian friend of the candidate, who is called their "sponsor," will guide them through this period.

The second stage is that of the catechumenate, which lasts normally from two to three years (there are exceptions). It is inaugurated by a celebration of entrance into the catechumenate. The ritual is oriented toward a first acceptance of Jesus Christ: "You cannot serve two masters, you cannot follow one without leaving the other," it announces, quoting the Gospel (Matt 6:24; Luke 16:13).

It also includes something original: the catechumenate community, that is to say, a small group of Christians whose sponsors and future godparents not only welcome the candidates, but also give evidence of their faith and commit themselves to accompany those who will be baptized. The latter are later marked with the Sign of the Cross over their whole body: ears, eyes, lips, heart, and shoulders. Then all attend to the Word, and the celebration comes to a conclusion in a prayer. During this stage frequent meetings are planned for prayer and celebrations of Christian formation with the catechumenate community and in larger groups.

The third stage is the final preparation: it begins with what is called the Definitive Call and corresponds to the time of the elect at Rome.

The Definitive Call normally coincides with the beginning of Lent for the Christian community, and the bishop presides: he begins with an invitation addressed to all to enter into a process of conversion. The ceremony consists, after several testimonials, in a statement by the godparents who speak for the faith of their godsons or daughters, and also a commitment by the catechumens who give (or "inscribe") their names on the list for baptism.

During this stage several scrutinies take place to make the individuals aware of human weakness, of the activity of the

Adversary, and of the victory of Christ. The formulas of exorcism, in contrast to those which have come down to us from ancient Rome and which were continued until Vatican II, no longer invoke the "condemned demon" but rather address themselves to God, for example in this way: "Free them (the catechumens) from the grasp of Satan who seeks to snatch the world out of your hands after having sowed there sin and death." The affirmation of faith called the "Rendering of the Symbol," the healing gesture of the deaf mute (the ritual of the *Effata*, the Aramean word that means "Be thou opened"), and the anointing with oil are suggested but not mandatory.

The fourth step is the entrance into Christian life with baptism. The ceremony, inserted into that of the Easter vigil, includes the litanies of the saints, the solemn blessing of the water with numerous biblical allusions and references to its fecundity, the renunciation by the catechumens of Satan, and their profession of faith. At this point each of them is baptized "in the name of the Father and of the Son and of the Holy Spirit," either by immersion or by having the baptismal water poured three times over their head.

After baptism, the neophytes receive from the bishop the sacrament of confirmation (which corresponds to the anointing with chrism of earlier times) in the most simple manner: an imposition of hands on all with a prayer invoking the descent "of the Spirit of Wisdom and of Intelligence, of Counsel and of Power, of Knowledge and of Filial Love, and of Adoration" (Isa 11:2), and an anointing with Holy Chrism on the forehead with the words "Receive the mark of the Holy Spirit which is given to you." If confirmation is postponed until later, the baptism finishes in the following way: after an anointing with Holy Chrism, the godparents hand their godchildren a candle lighted from the pascal candle symbolizing Christ, to indicate to them that they are henceforth the "light of the world" (Matt 5:11). The presenting of a white vestment is left to local custom.

Whether there are baptisms on the vigil night or not, the assembled faithful are invited at this time to renew their baptismal faith. Each one holds a lighted candle in his hand, and the celebrant asks: "Do you renounce Satan? . . . Do you re-

nounce sin? . . . Do you renounce all that leads to sin? . . .
Do you believe in God the Father? . . . In Jesus Christ? . . .
In the Holy Spirit? . . . In the Church? . . . In the resurrection? . . . In life eternal? . . ." He then concludes: "May the
all-powerful God, Father of Our Lord Jesus Christ, who has
brought us to new life through water and the Holy Spirit, and
who has pardoned all our sins, keep us by his grace ever in
Christ Jesus Our Lord to life eternal." Thus the Christian, sup-
ported regularly throughout his existence, on the occasion of
the annual celebration of Easter, by such repeated professions
of faith, advances steadily toward the encounter with his Lord.
The ritual concludes with a sprinkling with baptismal water:
it would be desirable to have a more substantial ablution, if
not a complete immersion. However, following that, the neophytes take part in the Eucharist, and there take Communion
for the first time whether they are confirmed or not, for access
to the Lord's Supper is contingent upon baptism and not upon
confirmation. After this occasion, the catechumenate community will continue to accompany the neophytes up to their full
incorporation in the parish community.

Today, in some countries, such as France, adult catechumens
are few, for most people are baptized as infants or small children. According to the "rite for the baptism of small children,"
one may baptize one or more children at the same time. If it
is several children, it is easier to assemble the parish community; if it is only one, probably only the family will be present.
In both cases the proceedings are the same: welcome, celebration of the Word with the intentions of prayer, blessing of the
water, renunciation of Satan and profession of faith, baptism
by immersion or by aspersion, anointing with the Holy Chrism,
and the presenting of a white vestment and the pascal candle.
Of course, while it is the child who is baptized, it is the parents and godparents who speak for him/her and who commit
themselves to the child's formation.

It sometimes happens that baptism is requested for a child
for purely sociological reasons, out of family traditions, without a strong guarantee of later catechesis. In this case the
Church reserves the right to postpone baptism and instead in-
itiate a period of preparation, a decision which is not always

understood or appreciated by the family involved. Even with such precautions in place, however, and because the question was raised by the altered practice of the Anabaptists in the sixteenth century, one may well question—especially in our time—the wisdom and even the legitimacy of infant baptism. We will bring this up again in one of the following chapters, for the problem is common to the majority of the larger denominations. Also, the number of infant baptisms is diminishing; more and more often it happens that parents, or even children themselves who have reached the age of reason, some even before adolescence, ask to be baptized. The Catholic Church is taking account of this development.

A "rite for the baptism of children who have reached school age," that is, from seven to twelve years, has been in effect in France since 1977. The process is the same as for adults: it is spread out over time, for the goal is to arouse the degree of personal faith that is possible at that age. A small community of children, already baptized or not, meets together with adult Christians around one or more qualified catechists. It is in the midst of such a group that the request, made by the parents responding to the desire of their child, or by the child itself with the consent of the parents and the promise of future support, is received by the priest.

Such a formalization of the request has the advantage of satisfying the child and its parents, but the desire of the child, the consent of the parents, and even their promise of support are not always the expression of a sincere motivation, nor a guarantee of perseverance. That is why one waits a little while before formalizing their entrance into the catechumenate. On this point the rite is clear, in that it inquires of the participants: "If we are here, it is to gather together for the progression of (one gives the names of the children to be baptized) who are beginning to walk the road toward baptism. To do that we will have to meet further in different groups: are you ready for this task?"

The celebration of the entrance into the catechumenate involves being signed with the cross, a proclamation of the Word, commitment by those to be baptized and by the assembly, and prayers and litanies. Afterwards there are more meetings with scrutinies before the day of baptism. Further, the small community will continue to live as a group beyond that day. The formularies provided are particularly well adapted to the situation. For example, here is a passage from a prayer for the action of grace: "Today we recognize still better how great your love is: you love us whatever happens, you love us in spite of our sin, in spite of our weaknesses and our denials. And that is why together we now say to you: Thank you . . . You have made us into friends of Jesus: place in our hearts the love that Jesus has for you." Here, as in the rites for the baptism of adults or infants, as in the rites for the other sacraments, there is a choice of "appropriate formula": one of the charisms of the Catholic Church seems to be to anticipate the various possibilities that may arise.

SUMMARY: *The Catholic Church, working within an increasingly secular society, has developed programs for the catechumenal preparation for baptism of adults and children who have reached school age, that is, people who are capable of professing a personal faith. . . It also practices the baptism of infants and young children.*

THE REFORMED TRADITION (CALVINISTS— PRESBYTERIANS)

The Protestant Churches do not have the same predilection as Catholics for anticipating the gestures and words of a ceremony, for specifying with rubrics—those lines in red type in the ritual books—precisely what one should say or do.

That does not mean that they do not have a "liturgy." This word means "public order": in a religion that means the cult, which is nothing other than a people's manner of behaving toward their divinity. At the beginning of Protestantism there was a liturgy by the reformer John Calvin, which has undergone several revisions; however, only in 1950 did a national synod adopt a "Liturgy of the Reformed Church of France," published finally after much experimentation in 1963, where one finds a ceremony for baptism, as for confirmation and the presentation of a child.

In the ceremony for the baptism of an adult, what is striking from the outset is the remembrance of the institution of baptism by Jesus himself: "All power has been given to me in heaven and on earth. Go, therefore, and make disciples of all nations, baptizing them in the name of the Father, the Son, and the Holy Ghost, and teach them to keep all that I have commanded you" (Matt 28:19-20). Also striking is the sobriety and understatement of the profession of faith: "With the universal Church, do you wish to confess the Christian faith?"—"Yes, Jesus Christ is Lord." However, the catechumen may still choose to recite the Apostles Creed. The catechumen is then baptized with the formula "I baptize you in the name of the Father, and of the Son, and of the Holy Spirit." The officiating pastor then asks the person to agree to the obligations which flow from this faith and welcomes him or her into the Church by inviting the baptized person to take part in the Lord's Table and in wishing him or her the assistance of the Holy Spirit.

There is thus no question of either a blessing of the water or of an anointing with oil, nor of the symbolism of light. This absence is explained thus: fundamentally, Protestants do not bless objects. However, certain pastors do understand the significance of doing so, like Michael Leplay who wrote at the European Convocation in Basel in 1989 on Peace, Justice, and the Protection of Creation: "When certain liturgies practice the ritual blessing of water, a rite which traditionally disturbs Protestants, fundamentally these rituals are professing the alliance between God and his creation, the protection of the living waters, and an ecological theology of the world."[1]

The liturgy of the Reformed Church of France similarly proposes a ceremony for "the Reception of a new member into the Church." It is here a question of admitting into full communion a Christian who has been validly baptized "in the name of the Father and the Son and the Holy Spirit" in another Church and for whom there is thus no need to be baptized again. This ceremony differs little from that of baptism,

1. The Unity of Christians, no. 73, January 1989.

with the exception that sprinkling or immersion with water is naturally omitted. At the time of welcome this aspect is recognized: "You have formerly received baptism as a sign and pledge of the grace that is in Jesus Christ, and you have been admitted into the community of the faithful. We receive you now as a member of the Reformed Church."

The ceremony for the "Baptism of a Child" also begins with the reading of its institution (Matt 28:19-20), but is immediately followed with an instruction on the significance of baptism "as the sign of our entrance into the covenant which God has established with his people from the beginning, and which, in his fidelity, he renews from generation to generation," as a manifestation of salvation in Jesus Christ through entering into his death and resurrection, an instruction in which is said: "What baptism begins, the Holy Spirit completes. It is he who brings us to birth in this new life; it is through him that we become members of the body of Christ; it is he who leads us into his Kingdom." There follows a celebration of the Word, and because we are here dealing with a child as yet incapable of expressing itself, the exhortation which precedes the baptism (administered either by sprinkling or immersion) is addressed to the parents. In the same way, immediately after the baptism, it is the latter who commit themselves to instruct their child in the Christian truth and to give their child an example of a life following the pattern of Christ.

However, certain parents prefer not to baptize their children when they are newly born; the possibility is then offered to them of "presenting" their child in the church (one also says "to have their child blessed"). The originality of this ceremony consists in underlining the commitment of the Church, which then "considers itself responsible for the child's Christian education" toward its personal fulfillment in the future, and which for that task requests the "help" of the family. It is also to cast a glance backward in recalling the previous occasion of the "blessing of the family" and a glance forward in mentioning the future occasion when the child will itself request baptism.

Whether baptized or only presented, when the child has become an adolescent and has completed their religious instruction, he or she is admitted to confirmation. The latter's ceremony is a little complex, for on the one hand it offers several variations and on the other hand must address itself to those who have been baptized as infants as well as to the non-baptized, some of whom have been presented in the church at birth and others not. Let us outline it nevertheless. First there is the announcement of the Law of God with the commandment to love God and the neighbor, together with the assertion of free will: ''I have placed before you life and death, blessings and curses; choose life, that you may live'' (Deut 30:19). Then comes the confession of sins. The majority of those to be confirmed, at least the youngest, are around sixteen years old: sin has already reached the point that the following prayer is appropriate (to be chosen among several available):

> Lord, we are truly sorry for having offended you; we condemn ourselves, ourselves and our vices, with a true repentance; we have recourse to your grace and entreat you to come to us in our misery with your help. Deign, then, to have pity on us, most good God, Father of mercies, and to forgive our sins for the love of Jesus Christ, your son, our Savior.

According to the Protestant tradition (which in this respect is different from the Catholic, which has the priestly minister of reconciliation, due to a different conception of ministry, say: ''I forgive you your sins''), the officiating pastor declares: ''May God grant you pardon for your sins.'' In the course of the prayers and readings which follow, there is a profession of faith and reference to the path traversed ''up to this hour when you are going to receive baptism or confirmation of the covenant of your baptism.''

In fact, the non-baptized who have only been presented as infants will be baptized with the baptismal formula, while the others will receive the imposition of hands in these terms: ''I confirm you in the covenant of your baptism, in the name of the Father, and of the Son, and of the Holy Spirit.''

By these words one can measure the difference between confirmation in the Protestant tradition and in that of the Churches which developed before the Reform. For the Catholic Church confirmation is a sacrament. Among the ancient Romans, the word "sacrament" designated the oath officials take, or the pledge of a litigant; it is not a biblical word. It was Tertullian, a Latin Christian writer at the beginning of the third century, who introduced it as a translation for the biblical word "mystery." The mysteries of the Kingdom (Matt 13:11), the mystery of the faith (1 Tim 3:9) and all the others are hidden and must be revealed to become known. Just as an oath or a pledge was the visible form of an invisible commitment or future obligation, a sacrament will be the collection of words and deeds accessible to the senses that render a hidden reality evident. It is in this sense that one asserts that Jesus Christ on earth was the "sacrament" of the invisible God, that the gathering of Christians, the Body of Christ (otherwise expressed, the Church) is the sacrament of the risen Christ, that the Eucharist is the sacrament of the Church.

The Catholic Church recognizes seven sacraments, among which the Eucharist, described as the sacrament of the Body of Christ (which is the Church) serves as the source of the others, in the sense that it contains implicitly aspects which they render explicit. It is in this sense that baptism renders explicit the gift of the Holy Spirit and the construction of the Church: "We have been baptized into one Spirit to form a single Body" (1 Cor 12:13). It is in this way that confirmation through reference to the seven gifts, the anointing with the Holy Chrism and the words: "Receive the mark of the Holy Spirit" renders more explicit this gift and this membership in the Church, and thus carries baptism to its perfection. Moreover, history teaches us that confirmation, at first connected with baptism, was gradually separated from it over time.

For the Reformed Church, confirmation cannot be a sacrament. As a matter of fact, the only clear divine institution in the New Testament is for baptism and the Lord's Supper. Luther made confirmation a simple ceremony which completes the instruction of the baptized person and prepares them to take part in the Lord's Supper. In his eyes the Holy Spirit is given in baptism, and the latter has no need of anything more. Calvin thinks in the same way: confirmation "is a fundamental insult to baptism, which truly overrides it and should render it useless. . . ."[2] However, he recommends making it a kind of examination: "a Christian teaching moment, through which children or those who have left behind their childhood should have to present the grounds of their faith in the presence of the Church."[3] The forty-sixth national Synod of the Reformed Church of France in Amiens in 1953 adopted the following resolution: confirmation "is the welcome of each catechumen in particular to the Holy Table to which the Church invites them. Confirmation is, for baptized catechumens, the occasion for a public profession of their faith, in which, responding to the effective word of grace pronounced over their life in the name of the Father and the Son and the Holy Spirit, they affirm, after having heard the Church's teaching, that they accept this Word and believe it personally." The resolution ends with the following statement: "Confirmation is, for the Church, the occasion for praying for the catechumens and to hand them over to the action, already efficacious within them, of the Holy Spirit. It is good and proper that this prayer, following apostolic custom, be accompanied by an imposition of hands."

Thus for the Reformers, confirmation is a ceremony in the course of which the baptized (called catechumens as long as they have not yet completed their instruction and have not been admitted to the Holy Table) profess their faith in the midst of the assembly of the faithful and understand themselves to be "confirmed in the covenant of their baptism."

SUMMARY: *For the Reformed tradition, the Christian is baptized "in the name of the Father and of the Son and of the Holy Spirit," either as an infant or as an adult, by aspersion or immersion. If he comes from another Church, he is not baptized again, but simply welcomed. A baby may be simply presented in the church rather than baptized. Whether they are presented or baptized, after they have been instructed in the truth and the Christian life, or later, they will be "confirmed in the covenant of their baptism" after having professed*

2. Christian Institution, IV, XIX, 8.
3. op. cit., 13.

their faith. However, this confirmation is not a sacrament. In effect, the Reformation suppressed confirmation as a sacrament for theological reasons, but it retained its form for pedagogical purposes.

BAPTISTS

In the Protestant tradition, an important Church is that of the Baptists. Deriving from the Anabaptists of the sixteenth century, they refuse to baptize anyone not professing their faith in Jesus Christ as Savior, and as a consequence they do not baptize infants. They baptize by immersion and not by sprinkling. What is their practice, and how do they understand baptism?

In a community like the Federation of Evangelical Baptist Churches, for example, it is practiced in the most simple and direct way. During the Sunday worship, the brothers and sisters to be baptized, already received into the community and instructed about the death and resurrection of Christ, are present in the assembly. Each one of them will give testimony concerning their past life, of their encounter with Jesus as their Lord and personal Savior, and of the transformation of their life by the Living Christ. The entire community listens to them with attention, sympathy, compassion, and admiration. The faith of all thereby becomes stronger, for it is a matter here of a proclamation of what Jesus Christ has done; praise then arises from the hearts and voices of all. There follows a profession of faith. It is in responding to the questions of the presiding pastor that those to be baptized affirm their faith in God as Father, Son, and Spirit.

The moment of baptism arrives. Each one, without other clothing than their white robe, is totally immersed by the pastor. The words that accompany the bath are eloquent: "On the profession of your faith before God and before his Church, into the death and resurrection of Jesus Christ I baptize you, in the name of the Father, and of the Son, and of the Holy Spirit." What is essential has been accomplished; certain pastors, however, follow this with an imposition of hands so that the Holy Spirit may manifest his power in the one baptized. During the exit from the bath, the assembly sends up to God a song of gratitude; and, in the course of the Holy Supper which follows, the newly baptized are admitted to the table of the Lord and take Communion first. That is how the celebration unfolds.

This kind of baptism is moving and fills the newly baptized with joy such that they will retain this memory as a continual constant point of light in their lives, lighting up the road ahead. Here is what one of them said:

> Barefoot, in a white robe (with no suit, no wallet, no wrist watch, no nothing!), I noticed that this made me think of an historical episode from the Hundred Years War: the burgers of Calais, themselves barefoot, in white robes, a cord around their necks, giving back to the king the key to their city. That day I returned to the King of kings, to the Lord of lords, the key to my life; and the most marvelous life that I could imagine began. He cured me, he saved me, he rebuilt my life, my person, our marriage, our children. He loves me, and I love him. I praise him as my Savior. Glory be to him!

As for infants, they also are received into the community, but not in a baptism: they are only "presented," and they and their families are prayed for, so that in growing up, they may find the path to the faith. "Let the small children come to me," says Jesus (Mark 10:13).

The unfolding of the ceremony of such a baptism gives a clear expression of the understanding that lies behind it. With the preliminary testimonies where each one says how he or she regrets a past life of sin and adheres to Jesus Christ recognized as their personal Savior, everyone understands that it is a moment of repentance and conversion for the remission of sins. It is an answer to the call of John the Baptist "proclaiming a baptism of conversion for the forgiveness of sins" (Mark 1:4), to the call of Jesus: "Change your life and believe in the gospel" (Mark 1:15), to the call of Peter: "Be converted and return to God, so that your sins may be taken away" (Acts 3:19). It is always the same call: Change your hearts, change your lives; believe! Repentance and conversion (in Greek: *metanoïa*, which signifies a change of consciousness) includes taking cognizance of one's condition as a sinner and being grieved by it, a taking account that leads to a double movement: a rejection of sin, and a putting of oneself on the road toward God. One makes up his or her own mind freely; and doubtless the Holy Spirit is acting in their heart, for the desire for submission to God creates a wish for baptism.

In effect, the Word has been heard: "He who believes and is baptized will be saved, he who does not believe will be condemned" (Mark 16:16). In the teaching of the Baptist Churches, this Word of the Lord is fundamental; it is the refusal to believe that condemns; it is the acceptance of faith which saves. Thus it is necessary that one believe; later, baptism should ensue as an obedience and a submission to the Word. Thus the baptism in water is not itself an instrument of salvation, but accompanies the faith of the believer, signifying and attesting to it.

It is an act of obedience: Having heard the Word, there is a necessity for baptism. Moreover, in carrying out this first submission, the baptized person is open to a total obedience to Jesus, his Savior "to be in a condition to oppose the stratagems of the devil" (Eph 6:11).

It is an act of liberty: the decision is personal, by some one who gives himself back to his Liberator.

It is an act of humility: Just as Christ was brought low on the Cross to be majestically raised up (cf. Phil 2:8-9), the baptized is swallowed up in the waters to rise up out of them and to lead a new life in Christ.

It is an act of faith, of affirmation of the faith itself: In proclaiming publically their Trinitarian faith, in being immersed in the midst of the community, the baptized witness to their membership in Jesus Christ, not only before humankind but equally before the celestial powers.

In this conception of baptism, personal faith must necessarily precede baptism. It must be said again: the refusal to believe condemns and acceptance of faith saves. Within the context of such a belief, "passing through the waters of baptism" is no longer an instrument of salvation, but an act of submission and obedience to the Word. Now, this is not the understanding of other Churches, notably not of the Catholic Church. For the latter, baptism is efficacious because of the baptism in blood of Jesus and in so far as it is an act of Christ celebrated by the Church: it is thus an instrument of salvation. Of course, to gather its fruits properly, faith is necessary; this, however, is a question that will be taken up a bit later in relation to the baptism of children. Should there perhaps be two kinds of Christian baptism, the one practiced by the Baptists and the other practiced by Catholics?

According to Scripture, there is the doctrine of *baptisms*, in the plural (Heb 6:1). Does that justify two baptisms? This plural usage, which is not used in any other passage in the Bible, is somewhat surprising; should one then understand that there might be a baptism today practiced by Baptists (and others), given ''in the name of the Father and of the Son and of the Holy Spirit,'' but which puts the accent on a preliminary event of personal conversion toward the remission of sins; and another baptism practiced today by Catholics (and others), given equally ''in the name of the Father and of the Son and of the Holy Spirit,'' but which is a means to communicate the divine life that God gives freely?

This passage from the Letter to the Hebrews has been interpreted in different ways. Some have thought that the Christians of Paul's time were familiar with the various baths and ablutions common at that time, particularly among the Jews, and among which baptism in the name of Jesus was unique. Others have suggested that many rituals were already practiced at that time, as they are today, before and after baptism, and one must situate within such a context the immersion into the death and resurrection of Christ. Finally, a third group, historians and exegetes (those scholars who study documents and who pursue the exact sense of a text) have remarked that the Letter to the Hebrews was probably not written by the Apostle Paul, but by some one else, perhaps by Apollos. But Apollos ''knew only of John's baptism'' when he taught at Ephesus (cf. Acts 18:25). He might thus be noting here this kind of baptism and that of Jesus, which explains the plural. There are also other explanations.

One thing is certain: "There is one sole body and one sole Spirit . . . one sole baptism" (Eph 4:4), and this is the foundation for the unity of Christians. Concerning this baptism, however, it is possible to have a "doctrine of baptisms" allowing on the one hand for baptism in water and on the other for baptism in the Holy Spirit, as appears in the Acts of the Apostles.

LUTHERANS AND METHODISTS

This work describes the Reformed and Baptist practices of baptism because these two Protestant confessions are well known in France and have two different understandings of baptism: for the Reformed, baptism with water signifies the operation of the Word; for the Baptists, it is a sign which indicates the union of the converted person with Christ. The Lutheran practice is close to that of the Reformed, and the Methodist practice is close to that of the Baptists.

For example, the Lutherans of the Evangelical Lutheran Church of France follow the following steps for the baptism of an infant: welcome, teaching (based on the Word of God with the Trinitarian development, and insistence on the fact that baptism was instituted by Christ), confession of sins, proclamation of the institution (Matt 28:18-20), profession of faith, baptism, a brief homily exhorting fidelity to these new commitments, and a concluding prayer.

One should note this passage: "We have been baptized once sacramentally, but we should be baptized continually through our faith; we should be continually dying and continually rising up. Our life as a whole should carry out what is represented in the sign of baptism." This expresses powerfully Luther's doctrine of the difference between justification and sanctification: the sacrament is the gift of the God who saves and makes the human being into a Christian; but baptism calls for extension and fulfillment in the life of the believer. For Luther, "Christian life is nothing other than a continual daily baptism, begun on a certain day and continued thereafter without end."[1]

---

1. *The Great Catechism*, Weimar Edition, Tome XXX, 220.

One can thus understand why Lutherans retain the practice of infant baptism, and prefer to call the charismatic baptism in the Holy Spirit a "pouring out" (or "effusion") of the Spirit.

In both Europe and America, Methodists have become much more diverse in their practice since the death of their founder, John Wesley (1703–1791); thus the forms of baptism vary from church to church. Even as early as 1798, adults and the parents of children "to be baptized, have the choice either of immersion, sprinkling, or pouring."[2] But the Methodist understanding of baptism is that of the Baptists: it is essentially a gesture one carries out to signify one's submission and obedience to the Word, with this one difference: for the Baptists, baptism with water constitutes one's entrance into the Church, while with the Methodists it is not necessary to be baptized to be a member of the Church.

The Methodist practice follows the doctrine of the "Holiness movements," according to which the first blessing accompanies conversion, while the "second blessing" achieves sanctification; this "second blessing" is thus in some sense one's true baptism in the Holy Spirit. In fact, French Methodists have reached the point of no longer baptizing children, but only adults who are able to profess their faith.

Summary: *The Baptist Churches, like the evangelical Churches which derive either directly or by adoption from the Anabaptists of the sixteenth century, have a distinctive understanding of baptism. Baptism is not an instrument of salvation, but only obedience and submission to the Word: thus it may not be administered without the preliminaries of conversion and faith, for which it serves as the sign. This is not the understanding other Churches have, especially the Catholic Church. However, there is "only one baptism"; and if there is a "doctrine of baptisms" in the plural, this should be understood in the sense of a baptism in water and a baptism in the Spirit.*

2. Thomas Coke and Francis Asbury, "The doctrines and discipline of the Methodist Episcopal Church in America" (1798) (Facsimile), Frederick Norwood (1979), 118.

THE ORTHODOX

We should have perhaps begun this presentation of the form baptism takes in the various Churches with the Orthodox, because their practices are the most ancient. However, we should note that the Orthodox Churches encompasses a variety of rites, as does also the Roman Catholic Church. However, the latter has one dominant rite, the Latin (which it has imposed, without excessive scrupulosity, on local Churches foreign to the Western tradition), and several minor rites in use among the Churches of the East in communion with Rome: these are the "Melchites," the "Greek Catholic" Christians in Arab countries, faithful to the Council of Calcedon of 451, and the Uniates of the Ukraine detached from the Orthodox and reunited to Rome at the end of the sixteenth century. The Eastern rites practiced by Catholics, non-Latin but united to Rome, are those of the Orthodox Churches which emerged from the schism of 1054 or the Eastern Churches which separated in the fifth century. Among these rites, the majority are specific to a nation with its own language and distinctive cultural expressions. One, however, which has generated an entire family tree due to its great age, does not have a national character and is celebrated in several languages, both by the Orthodox Churches and by several non-Latin Catholic Churches (specifically, the Byzantine rite).

Here is how the baptism of a baby proceeds in an Orthodox Church according to the Byzantine rite.

The sacrament of baptism is celebrated with lovely prayers of a biblical flavor and with ceremonies both before and after the day of baptism. Moreover, as with those of the Roman ritual, these prayers were perhaps invented and doubtless spoken orally before being written down and collected together for this or that occasion. They touch on the deliverance of the mother and her being churched on the fortieth day; the giving of a name on the eighth day after birth and the entrance into the catechumenate, baptism, and confirmation, the washings on the eighth day after baptism, and tonsure.

When do these ceremonies take place? As a matter of fact, with the exception of the prayer over the mother on the day of her delivery (for which there is a variant in case of a false delivery) and that of churching, all the prayers before baptism are made on one occasion: even the tonsure is added there, in the sense of offering to God the entire life of the baby: "Bless the head of your servant through my hand of a sinner by visiting him through your Holy Spirit, so that, as he advances in age and attains the white hairs of old age, he will render you glory and see the good things of Jerusalem all the days of his life."

As for the prayer "to make a catechumen," it follows that said at the bestowal of a name. The person to be baptized is presented facing east, head and feet uncovered, arms crossed. The priest prays over the person while laying his hand upon him or her.

If it is an adult, there will have been a previous catechesis involving a profession of the orthodox faith. In all cases various exorcisms are pronounced, with such expressions as the following: "In the name of Jesus Christ, . . . I cast you out, evil, impure, rotten, disgusting spirit. . . ."; "Leave this person who is preparing for a holy illumination" (those who are called the "elect" in the West are called the "illuminated" in the East); "look upon your servant, observe him, question him, test him, and remove from him any action of the devil." With gestures of support, breathing upon him, and signing him with the cross, the priest also says: "Chase away from him any evil or impure spirit that is lurking hidden in his heart (a formula that is repeated three times): any spirit of error, spirit of wickedness, spirit of idolatry or thirst for cupidity, any spirit of deceit or of impurity, any inspiration whose source is the devil." These are real prayers of deliverance or de-possession. There follows a triple renunciation of Satan and a triple profession of faith with the recitation of the "I believe in God," not the Apostles's Creed but that of the Nicene Creed completed in 325, that is, more developed and well known in the Latin Catholic Church, where it is recited during the Sunday Mass.

The ceremony ends with a prayer that is so lovely it should be quoted in its entirety:

> Lord our God, call your servant (one mentions his/her name) to your holy illumination; render them worthy of the great grace

of your holy baptism; strip off the old person, renew them for eternal life and fill them with the power of your Holy Spirit, in the union that your Christ has brought about, so that they will no longer be a child according to the flesh, but rather a child of the Kingdom, through the goodwill and grace of your Unique Son, with Whom You are blessed together with your Holy Spirit, who give life now, in the past, and forever. Amen.

On the day of baptism, the priest begins by incensing the baptistry which has been lit up: in the East incense has a significance which the West does not recognize. The deacon then pronounces a litany requesting peace and especially for a purification of the water, while the priest in a low voice prays for himself and his ministry. Following that, he blesses the baptismal font in invoking the Trinitarian God: the Creator: "You who have composed nature out of the four elements . . .": these are the four elements distinguished from antiquity: earth, air, fire, and water; the Redeemer: "You have come on the earth. . . . You have taken on the condition of men. . . . You have saved us"; and the Sanctifier: "You purified the waters of the Jordan. . . . ," "Come now and by sending out your Holy Spirit sanctify this water." This last formula is repeated three times, just as the water is exorcised three times through word and gesture (the Sign of the Cross and breathing): "May all the forces of the adversary be crushed before the Sign of the Cross." Finally, the prayer of the blessing of the water ends in the following way:

Show Yourself in this water, Lord, and grant to the one who is going to be baptized to be transformed so as to throw off the old man corrupted through the enticements of concupiscence, and clothe him with the new man, renewed according to the image of He who created him, so that, having become through baptism one and the same plant with You by conformity with your death, he may also become a participant in Your Resurrection, and that, having kept the gift of Your Holy Spirit and made fruitful the deposit of grace, he may receive the reward of his celestial vocation and be counted among first-born whose names are inscribed in the heavens.

Finally comes the baptism itself; it consists in a triple total immersion in the baptismal font with the words: "The servant of God (the name is mentioned) is baptized in the name of the Father (immersion). There follows Psalm 32: "Happy the man whose offense is omitted and whose sin is taken away." Following that confirmation is administered very simply, preceded by a prayer where it is said: "Give them the seal of the gift of your holy, adorable, and all-powerful Spirit, and the communion of the holy Body and of the precious Blood of your Christ." In fact, the Eucharist will be given to the neophyte starting with the celebration which follows (but to an infant only under the species of wine). An anointing with the Holy Chrism is made with these words: "Seal of the gift of the Holy Spirit—Amen." One then sings three times: "All you who have been baptized in Christ, you have put on Christ. Alleluia" before concluding with a litany for the action of grace.

SUMMARY: *In the Orthodox Churches baptism is administered, as in the Catholic Church, with sophisticated and traditional ritual prayers accompanied by gestures that are no less rich and meaningful.*

CHAPTER THREE

Questions About Baptism

THE BAPTISM OF CHILDREN

The practice of baptizing children who are as yet incapable of personally professing their faith is not common to all the Churches. Further, several of them (for example, the Baptist Churches) reject this practice. Thus the question is one of doctrine: what consideration could justify, or not, baptizing infants? And if one examines the result, that is, what becomes of persons baptized as infants, the question is a pastoral issue: does it make sense today to continue baptizing infants?

The Churches which baptize infants, called "pedobaptist" Churches (from the Greek: *païs, païdos* meaning "infant"), follow a tradition going back probably as far as the Apostles.

Scripture tells us that, at Phillipi, Lydia received baptism, "she and her house" (Acts 16:15), and the guardian of the prison, "he and all his family" (v. 33); that Paul likewise baptized Crispus (Acts 18:8) and remembered having "baptized the family of Stephanas" (1 Cor 1:16). Of course, nowhere is it stated explicitly that children were or were not baptized, but scholarship tells us that the term "house" at that time included the elders, the servants, even certain neighbors, and in particular the offspring, over whom the father of the household exercized an absolute authority, for children were considered as belonging to the father. It is likely that Luke, who wrote the Acts of the Apostles, and Paul, who wrote the Letter to the Corinthians, did not even bother to mention the baptism of children in these families, taking it for granted.

The most ancient irrefutable testimony concerning infant baptism is that of the priest Hippolytus of Rome, who wrote at the beginning of the third century with regard to the ceremony of baptism: "First one baptizes the children. All those who can speak for themselves will speak. As for those who cannot, their parents will speak for them, or someone else in their family."[1] In the middle of the century, Cyprien writes in Africa that "one should not refuse the grace and mercy of God to any person who has come into existence" (Letter #64, 2), and Origen in the East, the greatest theologian of his time, is of the opinion that "the Church received from the Apostles themselves the tradition of administering baptism to newborns."[2] Even if most probably at that time it was primarily adults who were baptized, the practice of baptizing children, attested from the third century onward, seems to go back to the Apostles and was not called into question again until the appearance of the Anabaptists in the sixteenth century, except perhaps by one or two sects in the eleventh and twelfth centuries.

It was precisely during this period that people began to consider more profoundly the basis for baptizing children. Lifted out of its polemical context, Calvin's argumentation seems solid. It consists in showing that baptism took the place of circumcision: just as the Jews belonged to the Chosen People from their birth in virtue of the Covenant between God and his people, in the same way the children of Christian parents belong to the Church in virtue of the same Covenant signified and brought into existence through baptism: "We thus know that circumcision contained a spiritual promise for the Fathers, and that it is the same as that of baptism, in signifying the remission of their sins and the mortification of their flesh, to live in justice."[3] So true is this that, for the Apostle Paul, children born to Christian parents, even if only one of them is Christian, are born "holy" (1 Cor 7:14). There is nothing extraordinary here: at this time children and parents formed a single being, according to the anthropology of the Semites. Cal-

---

1. *The Apostolic Tradition,* ch. 21.
2. *Commentary on the Letter of Paul to the Romans,* 1, 5, 9.
3. *The Christian Institution,* IV, XVI, 3.

vin further supports his position with this quotation from Scripture: "And in fact, just as the children of the Jews were said to be "a holy progeny" because they were inheritors of this Covenant, and were kept apart (separated) from the children of infidels and idolaters, for the same reason the children of Christians are called "holy," even if they are the offspring only of a father who is faithful (belonging to Christ) or a mother, and they are differentiated from others according to the testimony of Scripture (1 Cor 7:14)."[4] As for the argument according to which "one cannot show that an infant was never baptized by the Apostles," Calvin responds in the following way:

> "We do not wish to claim that they (the apostles) did not baptize them, since children are never excluded when some mention is made that an entire family was baptized" (cf. Acts 16:15 and 33). With a like argument we could propose that women should not be admitted to the Lord's Supper, since there is no explicit mention that they ever communicated in the time of the Apostles.[5]

And if one still objects that circumcision is not comparable to baptism, he answers that, according to Colossians 2:11, the sign of baptism and that of circumcision are equally "spiritual": "What is the meaning of this passage, if not that the carrying out of baptism is the carrying out of circumcision, inasmuch as the two signify the same thing" (specifically, inclusion in the Covenant). "For he (Paul) wishes to show that baptism is for Christians what circumcision formerly was to the Jews."[6]

The pedobaptist Churches thus have a doctrinal foundation for baptizing children: the divine life is a gift which can be transmitted to children just as can human life; it has its source in the baptism in blood of Jesus, an event which, from that point on, precedes our human birth. It may with perfect justification be deposited with the child like a germ even before its acceptance of the faith. For this germ to produce fruit, however, such a personal acceptance is equally necessary; but it

4. *op. cit.*, 6.
5. *op. cit.*, 8.
6. *op. cit.*, 8.

may come later. In this regard it is interesting to note that even "the Churches where infant baptism is not the practice" admit that "the gift of God precedes and renders possible its human acceptance" and affirm that "God's grace acts before we are consciously aware of it." They equally recognize that "in the missionary context of the apostolic generation of the Church. . . , Christian initiation included such things as the proclamation of the Gospel, *metanoïa*, baptism with water, and the reception of the Holy Spirit." But these Churches are no longer in agreement with those which baptize infants "on the relations between these various components, nor on the order according to which they can or should succeed one another." These quotations are from the "Final Report" of the first series of meetings (1972–76) "on the dialogue between the Secretariat for the Unity of Christians of the Catholic Church and the directors of various Pentecostal Churches and members of the Pentecostal movement in the Protestant and Anglican Churches."[7]

It is precisely because these Churches no longer agree that one may alter the sequence "faith-conversion-baptism" that they object to infant baptism and no longer practice it. The Savior's word: "He who believes and is baptized will be saved; he who does not believe will be condemned" (Mark 16:16) appears to them clear and unequivocal, entailing that a personal faith and conversion are necessary preliminaries to baptism. Confronted with this saying understood as an order to which one must submit oneself and obey, the pedobaptists bestow baptism on infants "in the faith of the Church," that is, basing it on the faith of the community, of the family and parents of the child, making it obligatory for them to bring up the child in this same faith so that it may, when it is capable, freely embrace the fruits of the germ planted in it through baptism. And this is what appears insufficient, even impermissible, to Baptists and to the great majority of Pentecostals today, as it did to the Anabaptists of an earlier time. For these, baptism is meant to seal the faith of the baptized person who is committed to follow Christ for their entire life; thus, it is not itself the

7. Translated from *La Documentation catholique*, November 21, 1976.

instrument of salvation. In other terms, it is not baptism which bestows the divine life, but faith; what baptism does is to create a covenant with Christ and a relationship (in German: *Bund*) with all other Christians.

Luther and Calvin both objected strongly to this doctrine; and from the beginnings of Protestantism, the *Confession of Faith* written in Augsburg in 1530 by Melanchton, who here expresses the thought of Luther, condemns it. In the works preparatory to this document, the objection was made that such a doctrine on baptism reduces "the sign and work of God" to "a password and group insignia for Christians." And in the final draft one reads: "On the subject of baptism, they teach that it is necessary for salvation and that grace is offered through this instrument; that one should baptize infants as well as adults, because by this means they are given back to God."[8] Although they both admit that the gift of divine life is given freely and is not dependent upon the consciousness of it on the part of the person receiving it, the two principal groups of Churches (the pedobaptists and the others) apply this principle in two different ways to reach two opposed conclusions. The pedobaptists believe that because the reception of this gift does not depend upon the awareness of the person being baptized, this gift can be extended even to an infant in view of the faith of the entire community. However, the opposing camp responds that, even though the reception of this gift does not depend on the awareness of the baptized, personal (that is to say, not communitarian) faith is no less necessary to its proper reception. The two positions appear irreconcilable; we shall return to this topic with regard to the question of rebaptism.

Also, the practice of infant baptism today prompts an objection that is not doctrinal, but is rather one of the practical or pastoral order.

In a time when the family, the institutions, and society at large were Christian, a child baptized as an infant could have its faith awakened to the life in the Holy Spirit planted earlier and be carried by the community through the various steps

8. *Augsburg Confession,* article IX.

that mark the various stages of its spiritual development. But today? While earlier an option for the faith was a natural and almost effortless step, today the choice between faith and disbelief is a much more difficult and much more anguishing one. It is not the case that the adolescent today only has believers as role models—far from it! It no longer seems possible to guarantee a smooth transfer from the commitment of the parents and the godparents to that of the baptized youth coming into their adolescence, nor for the latter to find an easy way from their baptism to an act of faith. How do the pedobaptist Churches respond to this objection?

The Orthodox, it seems, are well aware of this objection, but continue to put their trust in the germ of new life which baptism deposits in the infant and which the Eucharist (in these Churches, one is allowed to take Communion immediately after baptism, thus even as a child) develops over time, through difficulties and spiritual combats, assuring nourishment and strength.

The Protestant Churches which allow infant baptism offer also an alternative to this practice: the presentation of the infant. Certainly the commitment of the parents and of the community to awaken the faith in the child, to raise it and educate it in the catechumenate, is the same. However, this option has the advantage of reserving to the child the free choice to become a Christian or not.

The Catholic Church is in a more delicate position. A certain number of parents, authentically Christian, are troubled by the common practice of infant baptism and have requested also to have their children merely presented, though this practice is just beginning. However, many other parents, who have personally drifted or consciously distanced themselves from the Church and whose faith is less intense, keep on requesting, purely for social reasons, that their infant be baptized. In such a case, the pastor ought to defer baptism and seek to reawaken the faith of the parents. He is even obliged to refuse to baptize in the case where there is an older child who is baptized and was not enrolled for catechism preparation, for there can be no baptism where there is no guarantee of catechetical instruction for the person being baptized. In spite of zealous efforts at explanation and the most delicate pastoral approaches, it sometimes happens that such a decision is perceived by the couple as a punishment, which provokes indignation and revolt, and leads to a more complete abandonment of their practice.

What should one do? The pastor hesitates to crush "the bruised reed and to extinguish the smoldering wick" (Isa 42:3). To give in is to perpetuate a bad situation; to resist is to risk precipitating a situation where good people will live outside of their faith. This is the priest's dilemma. Of course, any Christians who can speak to such a family could still impress upon them the seriousness of such a response. Here we are only trying to mention the problem. The desire to be consistent on this point, together with the failure of parents to request baptism for their infants, has led the Catholic Church to set up a catechesis for adolescents, as was mentioned above. Still sometimes someone baptized as an infant and having now reached adulthood will request to be rebaptized. What can we offer them? The following chapter will take up this question.

———

SUMMARY: *The practice of baptizing infants goes back to the apostolic age and is attested without the slightest doubt at the start of the third century. It is based upon a principle, specifically, that the gift of the divine life is free and hence does not depend upon or require the consciousness of the subject. The pedobaptist Churches apply this principle: the faith of the community allows the child to receive this gift as a kind of seed; later, carried on the faith of the community, the child will be able to freely harvest and accept the fruits of this gift.*

Those Churches where infant baptism is not the custom apply it differently: one is not free to alter the normal sequence of stages, where conversion and acceptance of the faith must precede baptism. Further, in a society where one cannot rely upon the Christian community to carry the faith of the child to the point where they are capable of a free and autonomous decision for themselves, the question arises whether one may continue to apply this principle as do the pedobaptist Churches.

———

REBAPTISM

Sometimes people already baptized desire to be baptized again. This is the case where a person comes to the faith as an adult who was baptized as an infant but without any following instruction, either because the family totally neglected their obligation or because the person was not involved or did not respond to their catechesis; it is also the case with someone who simply feels called to live more fully their vocation as a Christian. It also sometimes happens that Christians already baptized leave their Church to switch to, or sometimes merely to join occasionally, another, and are rebaptized in the latter because their first baptism is not recognized. These are different cases.

A Christian who has received baptism as an infant but whose faith awakens as an adult with the conviction of having lived in sin, who desires from that point on to live as a devout Christian and thus requests a baptism that will be authentic in his eyes still cannot and will not be rebaptized within their own Church. The person should rather be content with repentance and receiving the "forgiveness of God."

The Reformed Church practices the "declaration of forgiveness." In the middle of the worship service, those present are invited to "abase themselves before God," after which the presiding pastor declares them "forgiven": this is a communitarian action, about which Calvin writes: "We believe that the ministers are ordained by God as witnesses and almost as pledges or surety to assure the conscience of the remission of sin, to such an extent that it is said that they may bind the sin and loosen souls" (Matt 16:19; 18:18; John 20:23).[1] A Christian who in this way comes to repentance is often prepared for it through a meeting with the pastor, a "cure of the soul."

In the Orthodox Church as well there is a procedure of repentance. It also consists in the free decision of the person to be recognized as a sinner, but above all it is a divine initiative and belongs to the order of the mystery inviting a person to enter into the secret of the mercy which God reveals. Just like every sacrament, it is a blessing. "The benediction," explains Father

---

1. *Christian Institution*, III, IV, 12.

Cernokrak, "is a gift of God, a revealed gift that man accepts freely and for which he gives thanks."[2] That translates itself into practice through a very beautiful action. The individual comes before the priest, signifying that he or she is a sinner; and the priest cover his or her head with the corners of his epitrachilion, the vestment formed of a single band enlarged into pleats at each end which the priest wears around his neck and which on both sides falls down to his feet (it becomes the stole in the Latin rite). His posture is that of the prodigal son of the Gospel (Luke 15) kneeling at the father's feet, as depicted in the famous painting by Rembrandt.

The Catholic Church also practices this sacrament: it is that of "Reconciliation" (still called by its pre-Conciliar name the "sacrament of penance"). As with any sacrament, it is an act of Christ celebrated by the Church; it bestows divine life, here rich in the mercy and forgiveness of God because it is an act of Christ; however, it does not bestow divine life to someone who comes to it without a sense of repentance, without a contrite and humble heart, "bruised and broken" (Ps 51:19). In the Catholic Church the accent is placed on the recognition of sin; the admission is made to a priest who does not declare, but merely pronounces the pardon: "I forgive you in the name of the Father and of the Son and of the Holy Spirit."

In the eyes of both Catholics and Orthodox, this sacrament has ancient origins. One discovers in the *Shepherd of Hermias*, a writing from the second century: "If after this great and solemn call (baptism) someone gives in to the temptations of the devil and falls into sin, he should do penance one time."[3] Once the possibility of forgiveness after baptism was granted, this practice became more and more frequent.

Today this sacrament is received most often from a desire for purification and, on occasion, for relief after grave sin. It takes on its full meaning in the case of someone who turns his life around so as to make a fresh start. Doubtless this is the meaning of these words of John: "If we confess our sins, as just and faithful as he is, he will pardon us our sins and will cleanse us of every iniquity" (1 John 1:9).

2. Read at the ecumenical meeting at the Ile de France, 1988.
3. *Preceptes*, IV, 3.

But sometimes a penitant Christian is not satisfied simply with recourse to the sacrament of penance. The person wants more, and something more significant or powerful: an immersion in the death and resurrection of Christ, a baptism by water which will be his or her real baptism, since the one received as an infant now seems empty of meaning. May the Churches offer this to him, since in their eyes baptism seals a permanent, unbreakable, and definitive covenant, and as a consequence cannot be received more than once? This question arises also for those Christians who recognize the validity of their infant baptism but desire to give themselves more completely to Christ and to symbolize by an immersion ritual the renewal of the baptism they received earlier.

An interesting initiative in this area has been made by the Presbyterian Church of New Zealand which

> responds to these requests for immersion with a ritual that expresses renewal while already presupposing baptism. . . . The person immersed and the congregation that supports him rejoice together at the grace of God, testifying to this grace that runs from the cross of Christ, which was sealed at baptism and that is being manifested now publically.[4]

This ceremony has been approved by the general assembly of the Presbyterian Church of New Zealand. Further, "it is made very clear in this ritual of renewal that baptism has preceded it":

> Long ago, even before you were aware of it, God called you, he laid his hand upon you, so that you might be his. Through your baptism you have been grafted onto the true vine, which is Christ; you have been integrated into the body of Christ. . . .

And the presiding officer states explicitly that he is strengthening the covenant with Christ, and not that he is baptizing. There is no question here of a new baptism.

In the Reformed Church of France such a practice could be encouraged to develop. It exists at Charmes-sur-Rhône in the Ardèche, begun through the "Prayer Union of Charmes." The

4. *Theological Renewal*, February–March, 1978.

latter, starting between the two World Wars with a revival in the Pentecostal tradition and initially guided by Pastor Louis Dallière, is an internal association of the Reformed Church where not only catechumens are baptized by immersion, but also those already baptized are immersed once again with the formula: "I confirm you in the covenant of your baptism." Although it has not been sanctioned by the Synods, this practice has been recognized by the National Council and been put into practice in several parishes.

As has already been indicated, the Catholic Church uses a ritual of renewal in the celebration of the Easter vigil, but the latter (most often employing a sprinkling, sometimes a washing) points less clearly to the death and the resurrection of Christ. An immersion would be more powerful in this regard, but the Church would doubtless hesitate to employ this because of the danger of confusing it with baptism; such a ceremony would lead many people who are insufficiently instructed to believe that that sacrament can be received a second time, while on the contrary this act has a unique and irreversible character through which God acts as Savior.

Entirely different is the case of people baptized in one Church who are subsequently rebaptized in another. Such a thing is not unheard of, for although all the Churches recognize one single baptism (Eph 4:5), there are some who do not recognize the validity of the baptism of certain others. For example, the evangelical Churches, Baptist or Pentecostal, do not recognize as valid an infant baptism or one by sprinkling.

Sometimes a rebaptism is due to the negligence of the party involved. There is, for example, the case of a Catholic who had for some reason given up the practice of his religion and fallen into sin, but who during an evangelistic revival of the "Full Gospel Businessmen's Fellowship International" (which invites people to lunch and calls them to a personal conversion), decided to "give his life to Jesus" and received at that moment deep joy and peace. This person was subsequently immersed at a Baptist church, and now testifies: "No one told me about the possibility of baptism by water through immersion for adults. . . . I was baptized by immersion without being bothered in the least about my baptism as an infant."

Most often, however, the need to be rebaptized comes from a different understanding of baptism.

The Catholic Church never rebaptizes a Christian who has already been baptized with water in the Holy Trinity.

The Orthodox Church in principle does not rebaptize a Christian who wishes to become Orthodox. This decision goes back to a council in 692 (at which time there were already separated Churches), where the parties agreed to receive a Christian only through the rite of anointing with chrism, a compromise to which, however, the Catholics objected because of the connection between baptism and anointing with chrism, but which the Orthodox held to; today, however, several Orthodox Churches accept such a person with only confession and the Eucharist. But a part of the Greek Orthodox Church, including Cyprus, Jerusalem, and Mount Athos, committed as they are to a triple immersion followed by anointing with chrism, rebaptize, holding that such a practice is not overly aggressive toward other Churches, but rather is consistent with their own understanding of immersion and their own spirituality. The Orthodox profession of faith, on the contrary, is obligatory in all their Churches.

The Churches which do not recognize infant baptism have a similar motivation. Thus, the "Final Report in the Catholic-Pentecostal Dialogue" already quoted above states: "To rebaptize in the strict sense of this word appears unacceptable to all. However, the participants in this dialogue who reject infant baptism have explained that they do not consider the baptism of a believing adult who received baptism as a child to be a rebaptism. This serious ecumenical problem requires further study."[5] Such a study is in progress; doubtless it will lead to the deeper realization that people interpret the Scriptures differently.

This disagreement is based on two opposed readings of the Word of God.

For the Pentecostals, one must understand Holy Scripture by remaining firmly attached to the literal meaning of the terms. This position has led one of their pastors, for example,

---

5. *Documentation Catholique*, November 21, 1976.

to the following teaching with regard to baptism: "Jesus says clearly that a person can only be baptized after having come to believe and having submitted himself to God" (Mark 16:36). This is evidently beyond the competence of an infant. Consider the case of Crispus and of the Corinthians (cf. Acts 18:8). The Ethiopian eunuch was baptized by Philip by the side of the road (cf. Acts 8:36-39). Verse 38 states that they both went down into the water. Thus it could not have consisted in this case of a simple sprinkling, but rather of a baptism by complete immersion. We have here a very clear indication of the manner in which a person should be baptized."[6]

In the Catholic perspective, one must consider two things. First, that the Holy Spirit has inspired the authors of the different books of the Bible in working on their intelligence to grasp the divine truth, on their will to write it down faithfully, and on their powers of expression so that they might do so without serious error (Letter of Pope Benedict XV in 1920), in such a way that this same Holy Spirit is the authentic author of the totality of these books. In the second place one must remember that these authors wrote with their human powers for a specific audience and that, as a result, these books have to be interpreted to uncover their true meaning.

This interpretation is in no sense capricious or arbitrary. On the one hand it will take account of the fact that the book is inspired, and thus must be inserted within the complex of books of the Bible. On the other hand, it will take account of the fact that it is the work of an author whom one must situate within the context of his language and culture, and, what's more, whose text may have been edited or modified by later redactors, who themselves are situated within a certain historical context and who are working within an established literary genre. Thus the labor of such an interpretation does not and cannot fall on the shoulders of each of the faithful, but must fall on the Church as a whole, on the totality of the faithful (among whom, however, certain ones have a ministry of interpretation), in virtue of the gifts that Christ has given them, a grace (in Greek, a charism; otherwise expressed, a certain

6. Vincent Esterman, *Vivre pour Jesus*, Ris-Orangis, 1989.

form of the Holy Spirit's action). Has not Jesus said: "Who hears you, hears me. . . ." (Luke 10:16). Moreover, it is this grace that has allowed the Church to recognize which books are inspired.

In opposition to the Pentecostals, then, Catholics invoke this grace of interpretation to justify infant baptism as this was explained above. Scripture declares: "It is God's will that all be saved" (1 Tim 2:4), something that is consistent with the whole of God's plan. Paul's Letter to the Colossians (2:11) shows that the event of baptism amounts to the same thing as the event of circumcision, just as Calvin later emphasized. Scripture also relates that those first baptized were baptized "along with all their house," and history instructs us that that implies the entire family. The institution of baptism will be interpreted in the same way. The divine intention is clear: "Go . . ., baptize. . . ." (Matt 28:19); but the Church believes it can reserve to itself the modification of the rite, just as she has done for each of the other sacraments: in this way baptism by sprinkling began to be allowed in places where there was little water, following an instruction of the second century. "If there is not sufficient water, instead pour water over the head of the person three times in the name of the Father, of the Son, and of the Holy Spirit."[7]

There remains the fact that it always saddens a Church to see its members move to another and to undergo baptism again. That is why, while respecting the journey of the individual Christian from one Church to another, it seems advisable where possible to avoid having the individual turn their back completely on their initial profession through baptism, and all the more to refrain from contrasting what is better in the Church he or she is adopting with what is worse in the Church he or she is leaving. Further, one should avoid letting that person believe that he or she may continue to belong to that Church, while being rebaptized in another one that the person is freely embracing.

In the final analysis, whether we are baptized according to one rite or another, as long as we are baptized in the name

7. The *Didaché or Teaching of the Twelve Apostles*, 7, 3.

of the Father and of the Son and of the Holy Spirit, do we not consider ourselves as all members of the same Body of Christ? If the answer is no, then in the eyes of such people a large portion of those baptized must not be part of the Church of Jesus Christ; and if the answer is yes, then why rebaptize?

An anecdote will not give a final answer but may illuminate the situation. One day a Catholic priest asked an evangelical pastor: "I was baptized by sprinkling while still an infant; am I a Christian through such a baptism in your eyes?" The pastor answered: "From the moment when you were baptized in the Holy Spirit, you were." What is this thing, then, being "baptized in the Holy Spirit"?

SUMMARY: *Sometimes Christians come forward requesting, and ministers demanding, a second baptism, and that through complete immersion. However, it is possible to distinguish a confirmation of baptism given through immersion whose legitimacy may be recognized, and a real rebaptism, which is inadmissable. The difficulty arises from the fact that, as the Scriptures are being read or interpreted differently, what counts as baptism for some is not baptism in the eyes of others.*

BAPTISM IN THE HOLY SPIRIT

What is this thing, this "baptism in the Holy Spirit"? For baptism by water in the name of the Father and of the Son and of the Holy Spirit is already a baptism in the Holy Spirit, in the sense that it communicates the divine life, a spiritual life, a life led in the Spirit. However, except for the rarest exception, such a baptism is not followed by the manifestations described in the Acts of the Apostles when it treats of the happenings at Pentecost or the conversion of Cornelius (cf. Acts 1:5; 10:46-47).

Must we not inquire how the Holy Spirit operates in the sacrament of baptism on the one hand, and how it operates during the visible and public experiences described by Pentecostals and charismatics as "baptism in the Holy Spirit" on the other?

Since the expression "baptism in the Holy Spirit" comes from the Pentecostals, what do they understand by it?

We know where it comes from. The founder of Pentecostalism, the pastor Charles Fox Parham, was a Methodist and belonged, at the heart of Methodism, to a revivalist movement which taught and practiced the "second blessing" also called "baptism in the Holy Spirit." This was a matter of a rather emotional interior experience which the converted Christians (already born anew or saved) experienced at some point in their spiritual growth. Now this pastor, the director of a Bible school in the United States, examined the Scriptures to determine what sign identifies and authenticates a baptism in the Holy Spirit; he found that this was the gift of speaking in tongues. This was confirmed for him when one of his students began to speak in tongues while he was praying over her. All the members of this group then began to impose their hands, and all received this charism. It was 1901.

This way of praying, with the exercise of this charism, began to spread during the decades which followed in the new Pentecostal Church, which he founded, and which began to influence, not without difficulty moreover, a number of Protestant Churches and even the Catholic Church. The question we wish to explore is the nature of this manifestation of the Spirit.

To answer, it seems wise to begin by recalling how the Spirit communicates itself in the sacrament of baptism (and confirmation for the Catholic and Orthodox Churches). "The Left Wing of the Reform" (as the historian Baîton in 1941 described the Anabaptists and other nonconformists), where one administered baptism only to adults and with the necessity of a prior profession of faith, made immersion in water only a sign that seals a covenant already contracted by faith. Thus it is no longer baptism which saves; baptism is no longer an instrument of salvation, but simply a conformity or obedience to a command of Scripture. One presents oneself for baptism after conversion "for the remission of sins," just as the crowds came out to John the Baptist and just as Jesus himself conformed to this practice.

The witness of a Christian immersed in a Baptist Church expresses this very well: ''I heard the word: 'Let it be this way now; in this way it suits us to carry out all justice' (Matt 31:13), and I said to myself: 'If it was just for Jesus, who had been circumcized as an infant, it would also be for me.' Following that I experienced ecstasy for forty-five minutes: I saw myself shining with light at the feet of Jesus.'' In those Churches where baptism consists in an immersion in water that is certainly meaningful, but which is not expected necessarily to transport the person baptized into a personal relation with the Holy Spirit, the question of a second use of baptism with water or of baptism in the Holy Spirit does not arise. Moreover, the text of Hebrews 6:1 concerning the doctrine of multiple baptisms allows one to justify such a position.

Protestants, who from their origins have only recognized two sacraments as in accord with the divine will expressed in the New Testament, baptism and the Lord's Supper, were reacting against the dangers of magic which both the sacramental doctrine and practice of the sixteenth century involved and attached great importance to spiritual reality, to the necessity of intervention by the Holy Spirit in the sacramental action. The sacrament is the Word of God, which is invisible and which alone can save; however, it is expressed within a ritual of divine institution: for example, in baptism the visible actions are the bath with ''water which washes, and that through the Word (Eph 5:26). The only conclusion that one can draw is that the communication of the Spirit is linked to baptism with water.

Catholics insist further upon the sensible reality. The water of baptism and the words of the person baptizing do more than simply signify the cleansing from sin and the insertion into the death and the resurrection of Christ; they accomplish these things, that is to say, they bring them about, they make them real, for what the Church is thereby celebrating, Christ himself is celebrating and accomplishing. However, the absence of a proper disposition in the one baptized, who remains free with regard to such gifts from God, can oppose the efficacy of this action. In short, the Church celebrates, and Christ acts;

but this may all come to nothing if the individual is not prepared properly. It is clear that baptism is a sacrament of the Spirit.

The Orthodox (at least certain among them) are sensitive to another aspect of this situation. As one of their theologians explains; influenced by the West, we have recognized seven sacraments. But what should one understand by this? Orthodox theology would prefer to think of a sacrament as a blessing, as a gift which God reveals and which we accept freely and for which he gives thanks. Within this perspective, "We no longer care about the number of sacraments, but we believe that God reveals himself through the sacraments, that he reveals his mercy to humans and that the latter commit themselves to accept his revelations. . . . In the face of this synergy (or cooperation), it no longer seems a serious issue to discuss the number of sacraments" (Cernokrak). This theologian thus attaches more importance to clarifying the nature of a sacrament (in its capacity as a revealing sign of the divine) than to a definitive list of their number.

As a matter of fact, among the realities or the rites capable of revealing the gift of God, the Church is not at all preoccupied with limiting those which flow directly from the will of Christ and in which she believes Christ himself is operative; for it is to the latter alone that she reserves the name of sacrament. Since the twelfth century the Orthodox and Catholic traditions have retained seven which, in one form or another, place the faithful in communion with the death and resurrection of Christ, while the Reform retained only two. While remembering that, on the one hand, the Holy Spirit may manifest itself without making use of the sacraments, one must also recognize that various rituals or realities of a purely ecclesiastical origin may equally, in imitation of the sacraments, be accompanied by spiritual effects. One would say that they belong to the sacramental order, without being sacraments. Is that perhaps why certain Orthodox do not attach much importance to determining the number of the sacraments? Could it not also be of interest to wonder if the baptism in the Holy Spirit of Pentecostals and Charismatics, with its prayer and its imposition of hands, would not also belong to this sacramental order?

However, before exploring this question, one should recall the nature of confirmation which is retained as a sacrament of the Spirit by Catholics and Orthodox. The latter do not separate it from baptism. By contrast in the West, because the practice developed of baptizing the sick by sprinkling without immersing them and without the anointing with chrism as happened at the celebrations of Easter, because the priests had begun to baptize in the countryside where the bishop was not present, etc., confirmation eventually became separated from baptism.

What is important is to recognize what is distinctive about it: by arming the individual for spiritual combat and passing on the power of the Spirit to them, this sacrament is distinctive in that it signifies the construction of the Church and carries baptism to its fulfillment. A text attributed to the bishop of Riez, Faustus of Riez, in the context of the Council of Arles in the fifth century, distinguishes confirmation clearly from baptism: "In the baptismal fountain, (the Holy Spirit) has accorded the maximum that innocence can receive; in confirmation, it offers an increase of grace. . . . In baptism, we are generated to a new life; after baptism, we are confirmed for the struggle. In baptism we are washed, after baptism we are strengthened."[1] Confirmation is thus more especially the sacrament of the Spirit. Especially in the case where, as with Catholics, it is dissociated from baptism, does it not find itself in competition with the "baptism in the Holy Spirit"?

Thus baptism with water given in the name of the Father and of the Son and of the Holy Spirit is indeed the instrument of salvation that bestows divine life and communicates the Holy Spirit for Catholics, Orthodox, and those Protestants faithful to the thought of the first reformers; and confirmation, where it is seen as a sacrament, also bestows the divine life. However, for the "left wing of Protestantism," that is, for one part of the Churches issuing from the Reformation, baptism with water is not an instrument of salvation.

A good number of this last group practice "baptism in the Holy Spirit" in conformity with the instructions taken from

---

1. Quoted by Paul de Clerck, La Maison-Dieu, 168, 1986.

the Acts of the Apostles: they are thus attentive to the signs of the Spirit. These are diverse, but they all have the same source, which is the Holy Spirit. Among them, as Paul explains (1 Cor 12:4-8), there are the charisms, the ministries, and the activities. These charisms or spiritual gifts are nothing else than a certain manner of action by the Spirit, who can as well favor some one without great capacity as he can purify the talent of a person having impressive natural qualities. Paul gives a list of these (an incomplete list, for he names others elsewhere) of nine charisms, specifically: three concerning revelation: wisdom, knowledge, and discernment; three concerning power: faith (which is obedience to the Word), the power to heal, and that of carrying out miracles; and three of inspiration: prophecy or the capacity to transmit inspired messages, to speak in unknown languages, and interpretation, or the power to decipher the meaning of the latter.

For the Pentecostals, following their founder Charles Fox Parham, if a person for whom one is praying by imposing hands on him begins to speak in tongues, he is recognized as having been ''baptized in the Holy Spirit''; the manifestation of one or more of the other charisms are also signs of ''a certain manner of action of the Holy Spirit.'' Further, according to these Churches and those which follow their doctrine relative to baptism in the Holy Spirit, this was the baptism given, at the very least, to Jesus in the Jordan (cf. Luke 3:21), to those assembled at Pentecost (cf. Acts 2:4), to the converts in Samaria (cf. Acts 8:14-17), to the Apostle Paul (cf. Acts 9:18), to Cornelius and his household (cf. Acts 10:44-47), to the disciples of John the Baptist at Ephesus (cf. Acts 19:1-6). Are not these sufficient models for today?

However, one must discern more deeply to make sure this is truly the action of the Holy Spirit, for the apparent sign of a charism can be counterfited, and the enthusiasm and the emotionalism which frequently accompany them and are such as to impress the company may have purely human origins. Take the gift of tongues, for example. ''He who speaks in tongues . . . speaks to God . . . and benefits himself'' (1 Cor 14:2, 4). To tell whether this comes indeed from the Holy Spirit, must we not inquire to see whether this helps the person to grow in intimacy with the Lord and love of neighbor? For a tree is known by its fruits (cf. Matt 7:17), and life in the Spirit is known by the fruit of the Spirit, by love accompanied by signs of his presence, specifically joy and peace, accompanied by such manifestations as patience, kindness, and goodwill, and lived within the climate indispensable to its appearance and further growth: faith, sweetness, and mastery of self (cf. Gal 5:22).

One must also not lose sight of the fact that, wholly apart from speaking in tongues which at first impresses its beneficiary, Christians are called to build up the community, for "the manifestations of the Spirit are given to each for the benefit of all" (1 Cor 12:7); thus one can receive a charism and exercise it without being very advanced in the life of the Spirit; a prayer group, a small Christian community may include a number of people who have special charisms, without their being extraordinarily spiritual people. Is this not the comment that Paul made to the Corinthians? Also, a prayer group rather advanced in the ways of the Spirit may currently have fewer charisms than it had during the time when the community was being built up.

In short, there is room for a distinction. On the one hand there is the manner in which the Holy Spirit acts in the believer when he is building up the Church (and it is, among other manifestations, in this way that he acts in first setting up the charisms); but the manner in which he works in the believer when he communicates the divine life to them or opens up a way for them to grow may be different.

Does "baptism in the Holy Spirit," whose charismatic manifestations are, with the occasional exception of speaking in tongues, destined to build up the Church, also have as its goal and result that of communicating the divine life to the believer and thereby to make him or her grow in the spiritual life, as the sacraments do? If the answer is yes, is it not doing the same job twice, and thus a bit redundant? The answer consists in showing that the Spirit who is sent, comes, expands, falls or rushes upon someone, according to various biblical expressions, may also rise up or emerge from a person who already possesses it. The baptized person, whether he or she be confirmed or not, has received the Holy Spirit, as was said with regard to the sacraments; but that does not necessarily mean that the person has been seized to the depths of his or her being, to the point of having been transformed into a witness. But this is precisely what the Holy Spirit does: it grasps the believer so as to develop, gently or roughly, the gift already received at baptism or at confirmation, and to orient this believer's will to himself, the Spirit; one he makes into an apostle, another he turns to preaching, another he makes a prophet, etc., each one a witness in his or her own way. How does the Spirit set himself to this?

A theologian of the twelfth century put it well: God cannot change, but he or she who receives God can be transformed by the experience. When God becomes present to a creature, God comes to dwell invisibly within his or her being and also brings something new that is equally invisible: this new thing is nothing else than a participation in God's holiness, that is to say, in God's divine life.[2] God does this a first time in baptism and renews it in the sacrament of confirmation (and again through the sacrament of orders). Thomas Aquinas holds that this renewal may take place even outside the sacraments; if there is indeed a case where it is a matter of an ''invisible mission'' (a sending of the Spirit) to develop the initial gift, it would certainly be ''one which brings something new, such as carrying out miracles, prophesying, to willingly risk martyrdom, or to give up all one's goods'' (the same passage, response to the second objection). At the same time, this is a matter of the extension of divine life to new objects: a miracle, a prophecy, martyrdom, voluntary poverty; the sacrament merely intensifies the divine life in a person who has already received it (response to the third objection). But whether it is a matter of the reception of a charism or of a sacrament, one must recognize an intervention by the Holy Spirit. However, once the person is already baptized, it would be better to speak of a ''pouring out of the Spirit'' than of a baptism in the Holy Spirit.

---

2. Thomas Aquinas, *Summa Theologiae*, Pars Prima, Q. 43, a. 6.

If one reflects on the spiritual journey of the Apostles, one can discern three great moments: the Last Supper, where Jesus delivered over to them his life in the very condition of immolation in which he would find himself the following day on the cross; the appearance on the evening of the resurrection where he said to them: "Receive the Holy Spirit"; and the event at Pentecost where the Spirit was poured out upon them to give them the divine strength and which also produced the various types of charism.

In the same way cannot the Christian receive the divine life at baptism (and more particularly the strength of the Holy Spirit at confirmation), and later become the object of a pouring out of the Spirit? This pouring out of the Spirit would thus be nothing more than the fulfillment of the gift received at baptism and confirmation. "It is not a matter of a repetition or of the production of a distinct or independent event, but rather of the insertion of an event, as it has occurred on one occasion, into another moment and another place within human history."[3]

There is thus no competition between the sacrament which gives or increases the divine life, and the pouring out of the Spirit which takes its source in this life to extract new effects from it. Thus if a baptized person, confirmed or not, kneels down and if his or her brothers and sisters pray with and over the person that the Spirit may come, this same Spirit, if the prayer is heeded, may renew that person (otherwise expressed, may bring to his or her being something new with regard to the life in the Spirit already possessed) increasing the intensity of the divine life in him or her in the same way as happens in the sacraments and also in the so-called "sacramentals," and extending this life to charisms for whose exercise this pouring out is a preparation. There need not necessarily be any spectacular effects, but there must be the fruits of the Spirit.

Although no ecclesiastical decision has been determined about it, such a prayer for the pouring out of the Spirit in the

3. K. Rahner & H. Vorgrimler, *Short Dictionary of Catholic Theology,* article: *Actualization.*

Catholic Church would be classified as a sacramental, for it fits the definition of the latter under the law of the Church: "Sacramentals are sacred signs by which, in some fashion similar to the sacraments, spiritual effects are signified and obtained through the prayer of the Church."[4]

Should this prayer be made before baptism or before confirmation, or should the manifestations of the Spirit be produced before baptism, as happened for Cornelius (cf. Acts 10) or for an unbaptized brother in a prayer group who begins to speak in tongues, the pouring out of the Spirit is no longer the fulfillment of the sacramental gift, but it does constitute a call to receive the sacrament: the person who is visited with this gift will desire baptism so as to obtain visible membership in the Body of Christ and so gain access to the Eucharist in which are contained abundantly all the graces present in the other sacraments.

THE CHARISMATICS

Baptism in the Holy Spirit is in accord with the teaching of St. Thomas Aquinas. But Pentecostals on the one hand and Catholic charismatics on the other justify it in different ways.

The Pentecostals were born in the tradition of the "Holiness movements" of the nineteenth century, where one was expected to receive successive religious experiences. First there was conversion, then a "second blessing" that purified one of the "root of sin" and through which one achieved sanctification. In 1901 Charles Fox Parhan with his followers added a third "crisis" experience, in which they received the strength of the Spirit as a basis for witnessing and testifying, accompanied by speaking in tongues; the latter was called baptism in the Holy Spirit. (However, some theologians already called the "second blessing" a baptism in the Holy Spirit.) As for baptism with water, this is only a ritual in the course of which the convert professes his faith; according to this doctrine, the Holy Spirit is fully poured out only during the baptism in the Holy Spirit, much less so during the first conversion.

4. *Canon Law*, #1168.

Catholic charismatics cannot embrace this doctrine, for the Catholic Church holds that the Holy Spirit is given in the sacraments of baptism and confirmation. In their eyes, baptism in the Holy Spirit is nothing else than the taking account of the presence of the Holy Spirit and the experience of his burning wind that gives peace and joy and transforms us into witnesses to him. According to this doctrine. The Holy Spirit is fully operative in baptism by water and the sacrament of confirmation; baptism in the Holy Spirit is nothing more than a change of awareness of what occurs in baptism with water.

Consulting St. Thomas Aquinas permits us to show that the Holy Spirit may be received not only in the sacraments but also in the charismatic baptism in the Holy Spirit. In fact, St. Thomas holds that the experience of the presence of the Holy Spirit flows from an invisible visitation of the Spirit sent by the Father and the Son which arouses a fresh activity of grace. Baptism in the Holy Spirit is thus a pouring out of the Spirit (a very real activity of the Holy Spirit), which the spiritually developed at all times have received. Thus, this is not something new. What *is* new in our time, however, is that so many people have been baptized in the Holy Spirit with a manifestation of charisms, and in all the Churches.

SUMMARY: *Certain Churches attempt to distinguish "baptism in the Holy Spirit" from baptism in water, but those which recognize baptism in water to be a sacrament of the Spirit should explain the difference between "baptism in the Spirit" (more appropriately called a "pouring out of the Spirit"), and the sacraments of baptism and confirmation. This pouring out is a visitation of the Spirit which has for its effect a transformation of the baptized persons: to make them increase in the life of the Spirit and to prepare them for growth in the Body of Christ. It belongs to the sacramental order, without being itself a sacrament, and should be placed among the sacramentals of the Catholic Church.*

Closing . . .

At the end of this study two different understandings of "baptism in the Holy Spirit" have appeared which correspond to two different understandings of baptism with water.

For those Churches which attribute to the latter the power of conferring the Holy Spirit, "baptism in the Holy Spirit" is a pouring out of this same Spirit. It increases the intensity of the divine life in the person who receives it and expands this life to new charisms for which it is a preparation. Only Christ, baptized in the Jordan to signify and to anticipate his bloody baptism and to be consecrated for his mission, was unable to receive such a pouring out, because he already possessed the Spirit in fullness from his conception.

For those Churches which look upon baptism with water as only a sign of concession and of submission to the Word, and not as an instrument of salvation, it is "baptism in the Holy Spirit" which bestows the plenitude of the divine life received first in faith. Christ himself was baptized in the Holy Spirit in the Jordan.

These two understandings derive from diverse readings of the same Word of God.

. . . and Opening

Whether Catholic, Evangelical, Orthodox, or Protestant, this diversity should not keep us from together announcing Jesus as Savior, dead and raised up, from calling to conversion for the forgiveness of sins, from witnessing to the power of the Holy Spirit (cf. Luke 25:46-50).

Certain Churches have endured for centuries and are consequently a bit out of breath. However, they are not dead; their traditions should perhaps be purified, but not rejected, for they still transmit authentic spiritual riches.

Others have been born much more recently and are full of vitality, but they run the risk of ignoring, even scorning, their elder siblings, and of expending themselves in a liberty without internal support, in an independence far from Jesus Christ who has deliberately taken on the human condition.

The Spirit blows through both; does it not wish that they mutually nourish one another, the better thereby to proclaim the Good News?

Appendices

A Personal Testimony by the Author

I was already in my sixtieth year when some students, old friends of the chaplain's office for technical high schools to which I had been posted, carried me off to the Christian Center of Gagnières, where pastor Thomas Roberts, who was the preacher and founder of the Unity of Christians and of Churches in charismatic circles, presided over an Easter ecumenical charismatic convention. And there, not having an apostolic ministery, I began to make a personal retreat: it happened that the wife of a reformed pastor prayed for me in a small group; and pastor Roberts imposed hands one night on all the assembly that the Spirit might be poured out in their hearts—but I was not present that night! But as soon as I returned to Paris, I was filled with a great joy accompanied by the desire to tell everyone that Jesus loved them, and I rediscovered the grace to remain for hours in prayer.

At the holidays of the ascension, I was invited to celebrate the Eucharist for the students whom I had accompanied to Gagnières, and these imposed hands on me so that I might receive the charism of speaking in tongues. And in fact, on the Tuesday after Pentecost, when the feast of St. Dominic was celebrated in our monastery, I received the gift of praising in tongues in the privacy of my conventual cell. This peace and joy persisted in such a way that I rediscovered therein what I had experienced many years before on the day when I responded to my religious vocation as a prisoner of war, and also on the day of my profession in the order of St. Dominic;

but as this phenomenon of tongues was new to me, I consulted one of my old theology teachers. This person recognized that what had happened to me was authentic and advised me to reread the treatise "The Divine Missions," specifically the passage on "Visitations of the Holy Spirit" in the *Summa Theologiae* of Thomas Aquinas, which I consulted for greater help. I then told the Lord that I no longer wished the privilege of my position as chaplain, and to my superiors that I was available for anything. I then received calls to work in the context of the Ecumenical Charismatic Renewal. Today, the autumn of my life has become even lovlier than was the freshness of springtime and the ardors of summer.

The Pouring Out of the Holy Spirit and the Sacraments

A Message to the leaders of Catholic Prayer Groups at the Charismatic Renewal at Essonne:

Baptism gives the Holy Spirit and builds up the Church: *We have been baptized into one Spirit, so that we may form one single body* (1 Cor 12:13).

The same is true of confirmation; however, confirmation is distinctive in that it signifies the construction of the Church and carries baptism to its perfection. In earlier times (and still today in certain Churches and in certain places), it was called Chrismation and was given in the same celebration as baptism.

The Eucharist is the sacrament of the Body of Christ (which is the Church). It is the fountain of the other sacraments, in the sense that it contains abundantly aspects rendered explicit in the others: rich in the forgiveness received in reconciliation, rich in the Covenant signified in marriage, rich in the Spirit welcomed in baptism and confirmation, etc.

The pouring out of the Spirit does nothing more than cause the ''Spirit to rise up,'' that is, develop the gift of the Spirit received in baptism and in confirmation (for there is a large number of people baptized and even confirmed who have not had the experience of the burning wind which transforms them into witnesses (cf. Acts 8:16-17). When received after the sacrament, the pouring out of the Spirit is an actualization, that is to say, it causes the grace received in that sacrament to be felt more intensely. When received before, it is a call to receive the sacrament.

Proselytism

An Extract from the Dialogue between Catholics and Evangelicals on Mission (ERCDOM) 1977–1987 (Translation from *Documentation Catholique,* January 18, 1987):

We recognize that a firm conviction of conscience leads some people to change their denominational affiliation, whether it be from the Catholic faith to the Evangelical faith, or from the Evangelical faith to the Catholic faith, and leads some to try to convince other people to do so. If these things take place as a free act of conscience, without any attempt at coercion, we do not consider that to be proselytism.

There are other forms of testifying that we can designate as "counter-testifying" and thus as "proselytism" rather than as "evangelization." We are in overall agreement with the analysis given in the study document entitled Temoignage commun et prosélytisme (1970), and we will here emphasize three points made there.

First, it is indeed a case of proselytism when our *motivation* is indignation, for example, when our true preoccupation in our witnessing is no longer the glory of God through the salvation of all, but rather the prestige and position of our own denominational Christian community, or indeed our own personal prestige.

Secondly, we are guilty of proselytism whenever our *methods* are based on indignation, especially when we have recourse to some form of "physical coercion, moral constraint, or psychological pressure'': when we attempt to bring about a conversion through material or political inducements, or when we exploit needs, weaknesses, or the lack of sophistication in others. Such practices are an affront to human freedom and to human dignity, as well as to the Holy Spirit, who always makes his presence felt in sweetness and the absence of coercion.

Thirdly, we are guilty of proselytism whenever our *message* contains ''an unjust and uncharitable reference to the beliefs and practices of other religious communities in the hope of gaining adherents.'' If we believe it necessary to make comparisons, we should compare the strengths and weaknesses of one Church with those of another, and not put what is better in one in juxtaposition with what is worse in another. The latter results in giving deliberately biased and tendencious valuations that are incompatible with the spirit of both truth and charity.

Statement of Agreement

Extract from the Declaration of the European Charismatic Consultation, Berlin, 1988:

". . . we shall work together as brothers and sisters. We shall seek to establish relations between ourselves and to develop a mutual confidence. We will make efforts to make our communities grow in charity towards one another. We will support each other through prayer.

We and the Churches, denominations, groups, and ministries to which we belong personally are in accord on many of questions of faith and practice.

On certain points, this agreement is completely evident; on others, it is obscured by differences in theological vocabulary, of pastoral discipline or practice. We will work together so that this agreement may some day find a better expression. We shall be attentive and we will respect the different traditions according to which the same underlying truths may express themselves. Without compromising our convictions, we will try to express our agreement in a fashion that is acceptable to all.

There are other questions of faith and of practice on which we are in disagreement, we and the Churches, denominations, groups, and ministries to which we personally belong. It is the task of the Holy Spirit who dwells in the Church to resolve such differences. In approaching such points of tension, we shall place our hope in the Lord. We hope that the day will come when we shall be a single heart and a single spirit. We take account of our true differences in a spirit of fraternal love and of mutual comprehension.

We shall respect the convictions of one another on such questions. Without minimizing the real theological differences which exist among Christians, we will make every effort to treat these questions on which there are different points of view with attention and respect toward our distinct Churches and traditions.

Between our Churches, denominations, groups, and ministries, there have been periods of tension, of opposition, and of conflict. We wish to leave these times behind us, in the grace of God. In virtue of the call that we believe all have received from the Lord to bend themselves together to a common task, we wish to express our mutual respect, both for each other as persons as well as for the various ministries we engage in. We shall speak in a positive manner about one another, and we will help each other reciprocally whenever this is possible. If it should prove necessary to express a disagreement, we shall do so without a spirit of animosity, but rather in a charitable manner that will seek the edification and openness that will allow us to learn from one another. . . .''